**NIST Special Publication 800-28
Version 2**

Guidelines on Active Content and Mobile Code

*Recommendations of the National
Institute of Standards and Technology*

**Wayne A. Jansen
Theodore Winograd
Karen Scarfone**

C O M P U T E R   S E C U R I T Y

Computer Security Division
Information Technology Laboratory
National Institute of Standards and Technology
Gaithersburg, MD 20899-8930

March 2008

U.S. Department of Commerce

Carlos M. Gutierrez, Secretary

National Institute of Standards and Technology

James M. Turner, Acting Director

Reports on Computer Systems Technology

The Information Technology Laboratory (ITL) at the National Institute of Standards and Technology (NIST) promotes the U.S. economy and public welfare by providing technical leadership for the nation's measurement and standards infrastructure. ITL develops tests, test methods, reference data, proof of concept implementations, and technical analysis to advance the development and productive use of information technology. ITL's responsibilities include the development of technical, physical, administrative, and management standards and guidelines for the cost-effective security and privacy of sensitive unclassified information in Federal computer systems. This Special Publication 800-series reports on ITL's research, guidance, and outreach efforts in computer security and its collaborative activities with industry, government, and academic organizations.

Certain commercial entities, equipment, or materials may be identified in this document in order to describe an experimental procedure or concept adequately. Such identification is not intended to imply recommendation or endorsement by the National Institute of Standards and Technology, nor is it intended to imply that the entities, materials, or equipment are necessarily the best available for the purpose.

GUIDELINES ON ACTIVE CONTENT AND MOBILE CODE

Acknowledgements

The authors, Wayne A. Jansen and Karen Scarfone of the National Institute of Standards and Technology (NIST) and Theodore Winograd of Booz Allen Hamilton, wish to thank their colleagues who reviewed drafts of this document and contributed to its technical content, particularly Tim Grance and Anoop Singhal of NIST, Edward Tracy of Booz Allen Hamilton, and Kurt Dillard.

iii

Table of Contents

Executive Summary **ES-1**

1. **Introduction** **1-1**

    1.1   Authority 1-1
    1.2   Purpose and Scope 1-1
    1.3   Audience 1-1
    1.4   Document Structure 1-2

2. **Background** **2-1**

    2.1   Browser Anatomy 2-3
    2.2   Server Anatomy 2-6

3. **Threats** **3-1**

    3.1   Threat Sources 3-1
    3.2   Basic Threat Model 3-4
    3.3   Categories of Threats 3-6
    3.4   Threat Summary 3-8

4. **Technology Related Risks** **4-1**

    4.1   Client-Side Technologies 4-2
    4.2   Server-Side Technologies 4-8
    4.3   Risk Summary 4-11

5. **Safeguards** **5-1**

    5.1   Management and Operational Safeguards 5-1
    5.2   Technical Safeguards 5-7
    5.3   Safeguard Summary 5-12

6. **Summary** **6-1**

7. **References** **7-1**

List of Appendices

Appendix A— HTTP Request Methods **A-1**

Appendix B— HTTP Response Status **B-1**

Appendix C— Glossary **C-1**

Appendix D— Acronyms and Abbreviations **D-1**

List of Figures

Figure 2-1. Basic Components of a Generic Browser...2-5

Figure 2-2. Basic Components of a Generic Web Server......................................2-7

Figure 3-1. Producer-Consumer Model 3-4

Figure 3-2. Simplified HTTP Transaction...3-5

Figure 3-3. Entities Involved in HTTP Transaction Processing...............................3-5

Figure 5-1. Filtering Incoming Active Content..5-8

Figure 5-2. Constraining Active Content Behavior with a Software Cage...............5-9

Figure 5-3. Verifying Active Content Digital Signatures 5-10

Figure 5-4. Verifying Proofs of Active Content Properties 5-11

List of Tables

Table A-1. Summary of Available Browser Request Methods A-1

Table B-1. Categories of Server Response Code... B-1

Executive Summary

The private and public sectors depend heavily upon information technology (IT) systems to perform essential, mission-critical functions. As existing technology evolves and new technologies are introduced to provide improved capabilities and advanced features in systems, new technology-related vulnerabilities often arise. Organizations implementing and using advanced technologies must be increasingly on guard. One such category of technologies is active content. Broadly speaking, *active content* refers to electronic documents that can carry out or trigger actions automatically without an individual directly or knowingly invoking the actions. Exploits based on vulnerabilities in active content technologies can be insidious. The following key guidelines are recommended to organizations for dealing with active content.

Organizations should understand the concept of active content and how it affects the security of their systems.

The use of products with capabilities for producing and handling active content contributes to the functionality of a system as a whole and thus is an important factor in IT procurement and implementation decisions. Active content technologies allow code, in the form of a script, macro, or other kind of portable instruction representation, to execute when the document is rendered. Like any technology, active content can be used to deliver essential services, but it can also become a source of vulnerability for exploitation by an attacker.

Examples of active content are Portable Document Format (PDF) documents, Web pages containing Java applets, JavaScript instructions, or ActiveX controls, word processor files containing macros, Flash and Shockwave media files, spreadsheet formulas, and other interpretable content. Active content may also be distributed embedded in email or as executable mail attachments.

Email and Web pages accessed through the Internet provide efficient ways to convey active content, but they are not the only means. Active content technologies span a broad range of products and services and involve various computational environments, including those of the desktop, workstation, server, and gateway devices. The knowledge required to understand their security ramifications is extensive. Organizations are encouraged to draw needed technical information from the many information resources that exist and gain a sound understanding of the security implications of active content.

Organizations should develop policy regarding active content.

Information security in any organization is largely dependent on the quality of the security policy and the processes that an organization imposes on itself, including policy awareness and enforcement. As appropriate to their situation, organizations should develop policy for the procurement and use of products involving active content technologies. Active content should only be applied where it specifically benefits the quality of the services delivered and not simply for show or because of its availability within products. Both the consumption and production of active content should be addressed by the policy. A badly implemented, poorly planned, or nonexistent security policy can have a serious negative security impact. The policy should be stated clearly and consistently, and made known and enforced throughout the organization. Putting an organizational security policy on active content in place is an important first step in applying effective safeguards and mitigating the risks involved.

Organizations should be aware of the specific benefits they gain using active content and balance them against associated risks.

Active content has a history of increasing risks as well as benefits. Security involves continually analyzing and managing risks. A risk analysis identifies vulnerabilities and threats, enumerates potential attacks, assesses their likelihood of success, and estimates the potential damage from successful attacks. Risk management is the process of assessing risk, taking steps to reduce risk to an acceptable level, and maintaining that level of risk.

Security is relative to each organization and must take into account an organization's specific needs, budget, and culture. As new products are selected and procured, organizations need to consider the risk environment, cost-effectiveness, assurance level, and security functional specifications, in making their decisions. Organizations should also be aware of the interconnectivity and associated interdependence of organizations, and that a risk accepted by one organization may inadvertently expose other organizations with whom they interoperate to the same risk. Moreover, since active content is heavily oriented toward rendering information for an individual, their decisions may affect the citizens being served. Once an assessment is made, safeguards can be put in place against those risks deemed significantly high, by either reducing the likelihood of occurrence or minimizing the consequences.

Organizations need to maintain consistent systemwide security when configuring and integrating products involving active content into their system environments.

Organizations should be knowledgeable of the features in the products they procure that can be used to control active content. Products and software applications that handle active content typically have built-in controls that can be used to control or prevent activation of related features. Email, spreadsheet, word processor, database, presentation graphics, and other desktop software applications have similar configuration settings that can be used to control the security capabilities of active content documents. Such configuration settings demand scrutiny in light of past exploits. It is an unfortunate fact that many products are delivered with insecure default settings.

Network devices or other special purpose software should be used to supplement existing application-oriented controls. For example, firewalls can be augmented by gateway devices to filter certain types of email attachments and Web content that have known malicious code characteristics and to reject them at a point of entry. Desktop anti-malware software has also become increasingly capable of detecting malicious code signatures within active content. In addition, many active content technologies provide mechanisms for dynamically restraining the behavior of mobile code by quarantining it within a logical sandbox. Organizations should become familiar with available security options and use them according to their organizational policy.

1. Introduction

1.1 Authority

The National Institute of Standards and Technology (NIST) developed this document in furtherance of its statutory responsibilities under the Federal Information Security Management Act (FISMA) of 2002, Public Law 107-347.

NIST is responsible for developing standards and guidelines, including minimum requirements, for providing adequate information security for all agency operations and assets; but such standards and guidelines shall not apply to national security systems. This guideline is consistent with the requirements of the Office of Management and Budget (OMB) Circular A-130, Section 8b(3), "Securing Agency Information Systems," as analyzed in A-130, Appendix IV: Analysis of Key Sections. Supplemental information is provided in A-130, Appendix III.

This guideline has been prepared for use by Federal agencies. It may be used by nongovernmental organizations on a voluntary basis and is not subject to copyright, though attribution is desired.

Nothing in this document should be taken to contradict standards and guidelines made mandatory and binding on Federal agencies by the Secretary of Commerce under statutory authority, nor should these guidelines be interpreted as altering or superseding the existing authorities of the Secretary of Commerce, Director of the OMB, or any other Federal official.

1.2 Purpose and Scope

The purpose of this document is to provide an overview of active content and mobile code technologies in use today and offer insights for making informed IT security decisions on their application and treatment. The discussion gives details about the threats, technology risks, and safeguards for end user systems, such as desktops and laptops. Although various end user applications, such as email clients, can involve active content, Web browsers remain the primary vehicle for delivery and are underscored in the discussion. The tenets presented for Web browsers apply equally well to other end user applications and can be inferred directly.

This document may be used by organizations interested in enhancing security for existing and future use of active content to reduce related security incidents. This document presents generic principles that apply to all systems.

This guideline does not cover the following aspects relating to securing active content:

■ General security considerations related to Web servers and browsers[1]

■ Secure Web application development.

1.3 Audience

The intended audience for this document includes the following:

■ Users of desktops, laptops, and other end user systems

---

[1] See NIST Special Publication 800-44 Version 2, *Guidelines on Securing Public Web Servers*, for more information on this topic. The publication is available at http://csrc.nist.gov/publications/PubsSPs.html.

■ System and network administrators

■ System developers and Webmasters who design, implement, or manage Web sites

■ Security professionals, including security officers, security administrators, auditors, and others with IT security responsibilities

■ IT program managers who ensure that adequate security measures are considered throughout a system's life cycle.

This document, while technical in nature, provides background information to help readers understand the topics that are discussed. The material presumes that readers have some minimal operating system, networking, Web server, and active content and mobile code expertise. Because of the constantly changing nature of active content and mobile code threats and vulnerabilities, readers are expected to take advantage of other resources, including those listed in this document, for more current and detailed information.

1.4 Document Structure

The remainder of this document is organized into the following major sections:

■ Section 2 presents an overview of active content and mobile code and discusses associated security problems.

■ Section 3 discusses the threats introduced by active content and mobile code.

■ Section 4 discusses the technology-related risks associated with various active content and mobile code implementations.

■ Section 5 discusses the safeguards available for mitigating the risks and threats discussed in previous sections.

■ Section 6 provides a summary of the recommendations discussed in the document.

■ Section 7 contains a list of references.

The document also contains several appendices with supporting material. Appendix A lists HTTP Request Methods and Appendix B offers an HTTP Response Status table. Appendix C contains a glossary. A list of acronyms is found in Appendix D.

2. Background

The private and public sectors depend heavily upon IT systems to carry out essential, mission-critical functions. As existing technology evolves and new technologies are introduced to provide new capabilities and features, new vulnerabilities are often introduced as well. Organizations implementing and using advanced technologies must be increasingly on guard.

One category of technologies that has emerged in recent years is *active content*. Although the term has different connotations among individuals, it is used here in its broadest sense to refer to electronic documents that contain embedded software components, which can carry out or trigger actions automatically without an individual directly or knowingly invoking the actions. Examples of active content documents are PDF[2] documents; Web pages conveying or linking to mobile code such as JavaScript, VBScript, Java applets, and ActiveX controls; desktop application files containing macros; and Hypertext Markup Language (HTML) encoded email bearing executable content or attachments. Taken to its extreme, active content becomes, in effect, a delivery mechanism for mobile code. The purpose of this document is to provide an overview of active content, its technological underpinnings, and suitable security measures, so that organizations understand the associated security risks and can make informed IT security decisions on their applications.

Being able to download files and electronic documents off the Internet is a useful function and a common practice for many people today. Web pages serve as an electronic counterpart to paper documents such as forms, brochures, magazines, and newspapers. Although paper documents come in different shapes and sizes, they are composed entirely of text and graphics. Web pages can entail active content capable of delivering digitally encoded multimedia information or even an interactive experience enabled by embedded computer instructions.

Active content involves a host of technologies such as built-in macro processing, scripting languages, and virtual machines, which blur the distinctions between code and data. Electronic documents have evolved to the point that they are themselves programs or contain programs that can be self-triggered. Loading a document into a word processor can produce the same effect as executing a program and requires that appropriate caution is taken.

The popularity of the Internet has particularly spurred the trend toward active content. A dynamic weather map, a stock ticker, and live camera views or programmed broadcasts appearing on a Web page are common examples of use of this technology. Web sites are also increasingly adopting technologies, such as Asynchronous JavaScript and XML (AJAX) and Adobe Flash, through which partial page update transactions with remote Web servers or Web services can occur dynamically in the background—providing a richer, more responsive interface for users than a complete page reload [Mcl05]. Capabilities for Web access have also spread from desktop and laptop computers to portable handheld devices, such as cell phones and personal digital assistants (PDA), and Internet appliances. Like any technology, active content can provide a useful capability for legitimate purposes, but can also become a source of vulnerabilities for an attacker to exploit. A significant share of today's malware involves active content.

Many Web sites offer electronic documents that act in much the same way as paper documents—allowing users to access and view content, follow references to other documents, and furnish information by filling in forms. That is, Web pages delivered from Web servers to individuals via Web browsers impart an inherent document metaphor [Ven99]. The value of this metaphor is that people are familiar with

---

[2]   While this document discusses certain manufacturers' products and standards, it is not intended to imply recommendation or endorsement by NIST, nor is it intended to imply that the products and standards identified are necessarily the best available.

handling paper documents and can quickly adapt to using electronic facsimiles appearing within Web pages, since they understand the basic operations. One drawback is that the document metaphor is generally considered non-threatening and can lull the user into a false sense of security. Moreover, strictly observing the document metaphor somewhat limits the way in which Web-based applications function. In particular, non-textual content does not lend itself to paper document style handling. For example, streaming or continuous delivery media, such as a live radio transmission or voice communication, can transpire only as it occurs in real time.

Increasingly, Web sites are offering interfaces that move beyond the document metaphor towards general-purpose vehicles to provision electronic services. In particular, many Web sites are relying on user-generated content, including social networking, photo and video sharing, bookmarking, and knowledge-sharing. These sites are becoming increasingly popular, with many organizations deploying one or more knowledge-sharing Web site sites for internal or external users. In August 2007, a video sharing site was the fourth most visited page on the Web, while social networking sites were the sixth, seventh, eighth, and ninth most visited.[3] These Web sites are more interactive than previous Web pages, allowing users—both legitimate and malicious—to modify or add to existing content. This situation imparts more challenges to organizations that must secure their computer systems against potential threats associated with user-generated content (see Section 3 for more information about threats). Where historically the flow of information on the Web was from Web sites to the user, the advent of user-generated content allows information to flow freely in both directions—making it more difficult for organizations to control what information leaves or enters networked systems.

A wide variety of active content implementations are available for Web sites to deploy, including PDF, JavaScript, Java, ActiveX, and other technologies which are discussed in Section 4. Each active content implementation may require a different interpreter on a user's computer (i.e., installed as a browser component), further complicating the security configuration for organizations. Because each interpreter may be supplied by a different manufacturer, users have the responsibility to track the installed browser components and update them whenever a vulnerability is discovered. The lack of a centralized configuration management system may lead to vulnerable unpatched systems. Similarly, new versions of active content implementations may alter how the interpreter presents active content. It is not uncommon for patches to active content components to be incompatible with the active content generated by an organization's Web sites, requiring organizations to choose from one of two potentially costly alternatives: continue using incompatible and possibly vulnerable browser components, or update the Web site.

While active content introduces a number of security risks into organizations' computer systems, it is often impractical for security policies to prohibit the use of active content. Many commercial off-the-shelf (COTS) Web applications rely on active content—and many legitimate external Web sites, from news aggregators to online banking and research databases, also use it. As such, many organizations choose to examine and mitigate the risks associated with active content rather than simply disallowing active content.

---

[3]   The *Top Sites in English* from Alexa is available at http://www.alexa.com/site/ds/top_sites?ts_mode=lang&lang=en.

Language Interpretation—Code versus Data: At one time, the security risks associated with the use of computers were relatively straightforward. Instructions were distinct from the data on which they operated, and some hardware could even distinguish internally between instructions and data (e.g., using separate memory banks). Over the years, the situation changed; tools emerged to facilitate application development in higher-level languages in lieu of machine languages, generic applications appeared, hardware processing speeds increased dramatically, and, in many situations, the divide between code and data completely vanished.

One example of the merging of code and data is a script. *Scripts* are data files or portions of data files that will be processed by an *interpreter* or a *just-in-time (JIT) compiler*. An *interpreter* processes commands from a script and executes those commands directly. Without a script, such commands would be supplied by a source file and converted into object code (i.e., native machine instructions) by a compiler—preserving the separation of code and data. Many scripting languages are intended to be embedded in data, using reserved characters or keywords (e.g., "<" and "if" in JavaScript) to distinguish instructions from data. Interpretive languages range from lists of simple macro-type commands to complete programming languages. Rather than execute commands directly, a *JIT compiler* will compile the commands into machine code. By caching the commands and their associated machine code, a JIT compiler can greatly improve the performance of an interpreted language.

With the arrival of the Web came the desire to make static pages more dynamic by using interpreters throughout the system architecture. Today, most data files contain instructions that aid in the presentation or use of the data. Interpreters are ubiquitous: spreadsheet formulas, database query languages, word processing macros, and script interpreters are not only embedded in Web browsers and servers, but also are used as standalone development tools to forge applications from existing program components.

While these technology improvements facilitate computer use, they also can involve serious risks, which are often not readily apparent. Many of these risks are associated with passing disguised commands (e.g., using special characters) or unexpected commands to an interpreter. A program that uses an interpreter to process unfiltered user-supplied information may be fed a string containing special characters that appears to be legitimate data, but will instead be treated as a parameter for or extension of an intended command, or as a new unintended command sequence. Injecting commands into a vulnerable application for execution is known as a *command injection attack*. For instance, many web pages take user input directly to compose a SQL database query; through specially crafted input, exploit code can be inserted, resulting in a SQL injection attack. Some applications use multiple interpreters in tandem, passing the output of one directly into another, which further compounds the problem, since a harmful operation may be brought about and executed unobtrusively along the way.

2.1 Browser Anatomy

Browser is the generic term used to refer to software that lets individuals view pages from various sources, including Web servers on the Internet, which make up the World Wide Web. Firefox and Internet Explorer are two popular Web browsers that aid in navigating text, graphics, hyperlinks, audio, video, and other multimedia information and services on the Web. Although Web browsers support a number of protocols, such as the File Transfer Protocol [FTP], they rely mainly on a simple, request-response communications protocol, HTTP [HTTP], for Web access. The browser requests information from a specific Web site by sending a method request to the Web server conveying the Universal Resource Identifier (URI) of the desired resource (e.g., the Uniform Resource Locator (URL) of a Web page), client information, and content handling capabilities. Appendix A contains a brief summary of the available request methods a browser can issue. Typical usage mainly involves retrieving information from the server or submitting form input by issuing GET and POST methods, respectively.

Once the request is issued, the browser expects a response from the server containing a status code, meta-information about the resource, the content corresponding to the resource requested (e.g., the Web page specified by the URL), and an indication of content encoding. Five general classes of response exist, as indicated by the first digit of the status code. For example, most computer users have received a 400 series code, the 404 code, at one time or another when unsuccessfully attempting to reach a resource at some site. Appendix B contains a brief summary of the classes of status code returned by a server.

The representation of a resource such as a Web page involves control codes, normally referred to as tags, and data. Browsers interpret control codes within Web pages, which indicate the structure of the data (e.g., beginning of item, end of item) and the way to render it (e.g., heading, subheading, paragraph, list, embedded image). The codes may also embed URLs of additional information such as images, which entail further requests to the server to retrieve the information and complete the Web page. The control codes are the subject of intense standardization and include specifications for HTML [HTML4], Cascaded Style Sheets (CSS) [CSS1, CSS2], and the eXtensible Markup Language (XML) [XML1]. Browsers are designed to read such codes, interpret their meaning, and render the Web page accordingly.

Browsers inherently involve many different program components, both internal and external. Figure 2-1 illustrates common components found in most browsers [Gro05]. The component layering illustrated is only for discussion purposes and not meant to imply any structural relationship. Essential core components present in all browsers include a basic protocol machine for HTTP and other supported protocols; a means to navigate forward and back, reload content, and maintain history; a parser for HTML and style sheets; and a mechanism to layout and render content. The remaining components represent mechanisms that handle other forms of content. To some extent, the specific choices depend on the browser manufacturer. However, competition and market demand influence manufacturers to offer components having comparable functionality with a high degree of compatibility and uniformity. Interpreters for scripting languages (e.g., JavaScript, Visual Basic Script, and JScript) are a useful means of processing instructions conveyed from the server by the browser. Similarly, environmental components for Java, ActiveX, and Plug-in technology allow other types of code to be executed at the browser. Further details about these technologies are given in Section 4.

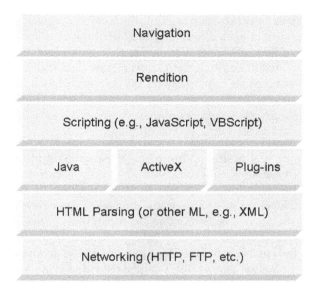

Figure 2-1. Basic Components of a Generic Browser

To simplify browser development, software designs allow extensibility through a variety of techniques for communicating with other functional components. The motivation is twofold: no one can reasonably build in the means to render all forms of content, and to attempt to do so would limit innovation as well as the usefulness of the browser. As long as the browser design employs or provides a well-defined interface, other software producers can readily extend functionality with their components. In general, the program components of a browser, both built-in and otherwise, can be divided into the classes described below [Mor98].

■ **Components incorporated directly within the browser.** Browsers contain a significant amount of built-in functionality and typically can inherently render a variety of content types, including text, HTML delimited text, scripting languages, Java applets, and common types of image files. The associated program components are functionally internal to the browser and able to interpret such content directly. To keep the browser safe from sources that have varying levels of trust, the program components must take precautions against arbitrary input received. Because these programs are contained within the browser, the browser manufacturer is able to impose security constraints on them. Built-in functionality is also a means for the manufacturer to distinguish its product from others in various ways such as offering proprietary extensions to standard script languages, close integration and interworking with other product offerings, and entirely new content handling capabilities.

Built-in functionality should follow an explicit security model to ensure security. For example, enforcing the same origin policy, which prevents content loaded from one "origin' (i.e., the context defined by host domain name, protocol, and port) from getting or setting properties of a document loaded from a different "origin," is a fundamental policy employed by present-day browsers. The implementation of secure JavaScript in Mozilla illustrates the range of considerations involved in defining a security model [Anu98]. The implementation controls access to resources and external interfaces, prevents residual information from being retained and accessible among different contexts operating simultaneously or sequentially, and allows policy, which partitions the name space for access control purposes, to be specified independently of mechanism. Differences can and do exist in the security models used by different browsers.

■ **Components installed to extend the browser functionality.** A significant innovation in the design of Web browsers is the ability to extend them beyond their built-in functionality through a defined interface. For a browser to hand off content rendering to such program components, the component must register its handling capabilities (i.e., the file extensions and Multipurpose Internet Mail Extensions [MIME] content types it supports) with the browser when it installs. Often, these extensions require full access to the browser internals and the underlying operating system (OS) to accomplish their goals. Programs that extend browsers typically enjoy full function interfaces to the internals of the browsers and to the OS.

The two most common means of extending browsers, Netscape plug-ins and ActiveX controls, have somewhat different security models. Microsoft ActiveX controls can require authenticated digital signatures as a prerequisite for installation, while Netscape plug-ins have no mechanism for enforcing authenticated signatures. Once an ActiveX control is installed, however, it has free range over the entire machine, whereas the plug-in is confined to the capabilities of the browser.

■ **Programs launched as independently executing processes.** As an alternative to using a programming interface, a browser's capabilities can be extended using a so-called helper application or content viewer. Like a plug-in, the browser starts a helper application and hands off content rendering when it encounters a content type (MIME content type or file extension) for which the helper application is registered to handle. Unlike a plug-in, a helper application runs separately from the browser in its own process space, and does not interact with or rely on the browser once initiated. Because a helper application runs independently, executed with the content file as input, it is completely outside of the control of the browser, including the browser's security controls.

■ **Components directly encapsulating the browser.** An interesting and somewhat unconventional approach is to embody the browser itself within another application as a means of extending functionality. A good example is Internet Explorer, or any other browser that complies with ActiveX container or Object Linking and Embedding (OLE) container technology, which can be run as an ActiveX control inside an application. Visual Basic applications inherently have this capability, which allows one to not only control the URL requested, but also interact with some of the content on the screen, or even allow HTML pages to pass information to and from the container application [Hug99]. Originally, Microsoft MSN, America Online, and a number of free Internet service access providers configured their branded browsers this way. A number of browsers developed using different technology schemes are available today specifically for being embedded within an application as a means of adding new functionality. An email application, for example, could use such a component to enhance its capabilities and render HTML-formatted messages directly, including any embedded scripts.

2.2 Server Anatomy

A *Web server* is a computing platform that supplies information and services to other host computers. The delivered content contains text, image, audio, and video information, formatted in HTML or another markup language. A Web server performs this function by responding to HTTP requests sent to it from a Web browser.

The transaction begins when a browser requests a resource from the Web server. In the simplest case, the Web server retrieves the requested content from a file system and transmits it to the browser. While this approach works well for static non-volatile information, it can be unsuitable in situations where the information is volatile, already resides in a database or other repository under a different format, or varies according to the input provided. In such cases, the Web server responds to the request by creating the content dynamically, typically by spawning a process or lightweight thread to generate the information.

The Common Gateway Interface (CGI) is an industry standard for communicating between a Web server and another program that is often employed in such instances.

As with browsers, Web servers involve many different kinds of program components and are designed to be extensible and to interact with databases, legacy systems, and other servers running on an organization's network. Figure 2-2 illustrates the common components found in most servers [Has00]. The key components present in all Web servers are a basic protocol machine for HTTP, authentication and access control enforcement, a means to fetch Web pages or resource templates, and a mechanism to compose and validate the contents of the response. Resource templates are similar to Web pages, but in addition to text and markup tags, also contain embedded commands and scripts that are executed to dynamically create the Web page content. The remaining components represent mechanisms that generate content dynamically through server side scripting or by other means. The specific choices for extending server technology with specific types of dynamic content mechanisms depend on the availability of compatible modules from the Web server manufacturer and other module producers.

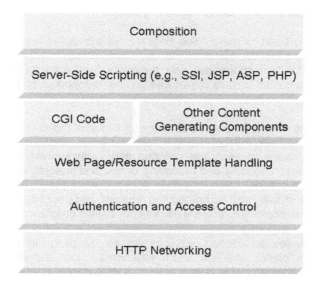

Figure 2-2. Basic Components of a Generic Web Server

CGI scripts were the initial mechanism used to enable Web sites to interact with databases and other applications. A CGI application executes as a separate process, which can be written in a variety of programming languages. As an independent process, the application is capable of accessing other hosts (e.g., a database server) and resources in performing its function, subject to its system security permissions. Once the application creates the information, the Web server conveys it in a response back to the browser.

One drawback with this approach is that it consumes a significant amount of computational resources to spawn a new process for each request. As Web technologies evolved, a number of other programming interfaces offering performance improvements have arisen, such as the Apache Application Programming Interface (API), the Netscape Server Application Programming Interface (NSAPI), and the Internet Server Application Programming Interface (ISAPI). Applications using these interfaces operate quite a bit differently from a CGI application. For example, an ISAPI application executes as an integral part of the Web server within the same address space as the server code and can remain in memory or be removed from memory dynamically to conserve system resources.

Server-side processing methods also have been developed that take advantage of these more efficient interfaces and are easier to program; for example, Microsoft ASP.NET for use with Internet Information Services (IIS) servers, Java Server Pages supported by Sun and Netscape, and the freeware PHP Hypertext Preprocessor (PHP) supported by most major Web platforms, including Apache and IIS. In general, the techniques for dynamically generating content and improving Web server capabilities tend to be proprietary and used by software manufacturers to differentiate their product from others in the marketplace. Further details of common content generating technologies, including Server Side Includes (SSI), Active Server Pages (ASP), Java Server Pages (JSP), and PHP, are discussed in Section 4.

Web Scripting – Client vs. Server: It is important to distinguish scripts run by the browser (i.e., client-side scripting) from those run by the Web server (i.e., server-side scripting). Client-side scripting and server-side scripting are distinct concepts that serve different purposes. For example, since a server does not interact directly with a user, server-side scripting requires no human-to-computer interface capability. Furthermore, the Web browser and server each supply their own unique environment for executing scripts.

Client-side scripting is used to make Web pages more interactive and functional after they have been sent to the browser. For example, client-side scripts might involve validating data entry fields on an HTML form so the user gets immediate feedback when a mistake occurs, or integrating an ActiveX control or Java applet with another component on the page so that they interact.

A Web browser environment for client-side scripting includes the objects that represent the user interface (e.g., windows, menus, dialog boxes, text areas, anchors, frames, cookies, and input/output) and a means to associate scripting code with events at that interface (e.g., change of focus, selection, loading and unloading of text and images, form submission, error and abort, and mouse actions). Scripting code appears within the HTML, and the displayed page is a combination of fixed and computed text, images, and user interface elements. Since the scripts react to user interaction, there is no need for a main program.

A Web server provides a different environment for scripting, which includes objects representing requests, clients, and files, and mechanisms to lock and share data. All server-side scripting takes place before the resource (e.g., a Web page) is sent to the browser. The server-side scripts, for example, may involve creating a Web page dynamically by querying a database and formatting the results into HTML for delivery to the browser.

By using both client-side and server-side scripting in a Web-based application, it is possible to distribute processing effectively between the browser and Web server, while providing a customized user interface.

Client-side scripting depends on the browser that processes a script, which requires awareness of the capabilities of browsers that might be encountered. While server-side scripting, such as with ASP pages, can create pure HTML pages acceptable by any browser, they are not necessarily portable to or compatible with the Web server software running elsewhere in an organization.

---

3. Threats

Threats are possible dangers to a computer system, which may result in the interception, alteration, obstruction, destruction, or other disruption of computational resources. Understanding the nature of the threats associated with active content and mobile code is the first step towards reducing them. Reducing threats minimizes the possibility of attacks, which are the realizations of specific threats that impact the confidentiality, integrity, accountability, or availability of a computational resource.

3.1 Threat Sources

Organizations' increasing reliance on networked computing systems for critical functions has revealed a number of shortcomings in the original design of the networking protocols in use on the Internet. While some security features were foreseen and built into these protocols, a number of others were not addressed, including:

■ **Data confidentiality.** Data passed across the Internet using the Internet Protocol (IP) travel in packets that can be captured easily and viewed to reveal their contents.

■ **Data integrity.** Data traversing the Internet may be intercepted and modified before reaching the recipient or replayed later. While IP provides a limited checksum feature, it is not cryptographically bound to data packets and can be modified easily.

■ **User identification and authentication.** IP packets do not provide user identification or authentication. Due to the layered model of the Internet, the responsibility for user authentication falls to the application layer protocol (e.g., HTTP [HTTP], Simple Mail Transfer Protocol [SMTP], FTP [FTP]). Unfortunately, many of these protocols rely on cleartext passwords, which are susceptible to being captured by eavesdroppers.

■ **System identification and authentication.** IP packets contain Internet addresses identifying the host or gateway system that sent the packet, but these addresses are not protected (e.g., by cryptography) and can easily be spoofed.

■ **Reliable domain name translation.** The Domain Name System (DNS) used to translate names to host addresses on the Internet relies on truthful and accurate reporting of mappings by all components, which is difficult to ensure. DNS was not designed to provide integrity or authentication services.

■ **Mobile code security.** Many Web sites supply code that the Web browser must process. Some of the most common forms of mobile code are JavaScript, Asynchronous JavaScript and XML (AJAX), Java applets, ActiveX, and Flash. Each form of mobile code has a different security model and configuration management process, increasing the complexity of securing mobile code hosts and the code itself.

These omissions provide one source of vulnerabilities intruders use to devise attacks against hosts on the Internet. Other vulnerabilities in an operating system, Web server software, or a Web protocol may also be present in many, if not most, Web sites at a given time, creating further opportunity for attack. The nature of the Internet amplifies the risks associated with vulnerabilities in connected hosts. Many initiatives to mitigate threats are underway or reaching maturity. Standards for Internet Protocol Security (IPsec), Secure DNS, and Public Key Infrastructure (PKI) have been implemented in products. Government-certified security evaluation laboratories have been established under regional and worldwide mutual recognition schemes. Organizations have established incident response teams, which have improved their effectiveness in combating intrusions. Commercial software for detecting and eliminating malware, filtering network protocols, patching computer systems, and detecting and preventing intrusions is widely available. While the outlook should be positive due to these advancements, a number of factors contribute to perpetuating security problems, particularly those summarized below.

3.1.1 Scale of the Internet

Millions of computers make up the Internet. Its vast scale precludes wholesale upgrades to new security protocols and solutions. As a result, a large pool of systems lags in various degrees from having the most current protection mechanisms in place. While a single organization's network may have up-to-date and secure systems, one or more systems from the pool of stragglers may be used as a launch pad for new attacks individually or as part of a coordinated group of systems called a *botnet* [McC03]. Members of a botnet are typically poorly secured desktop or laptop computers with high-speed Internet connectivity on which programs to cause them to attack other systems have been surreptitiously installed. A study done in 2006 of about 4.5 million URLs found that, at a minimum, 10 percent of them were engaging in surreptitious downloads of malicious code [Pro07].

3.1.2 Window of Exposure

Errors of commission or omission invariably occur that create vulnerabilities that allow protection mechanisms to be bypassed or disabled. An individual vulnerability may not pose a serious problem, depending on such factors as the level of access and complexity of the attack needed to exploit the vulnerability and the availability of exploit code or tools. As vulnerabilities are discovered and made known to the manufacturer, a window of exposure exists until a patch containing corrective code to close the vulnerability is made available. A patch usually involves the installation of native, platform-specific code modules, which are developed as a replacement for or an insertion into compiled code that is already installed on a computer. Any delay in applying the patch opens the window not only to a wider time period for exploitation, but also to a greater audience of potential intruders, as attack tools that exploit the vulnerability emerge. Today, vulnerabilities are discovered at an increasingly high frequency, further aggravating the problem. In fact, it is not uncommon for exploits to be available before the vulnerability is publicly announced or acknowledged by the software's manufacturer; these are known as *zero-day exploits*.

3.1.3 Quality of Software Products

Software products often contain large numbers of unintentional implementation errors. Modern market-driven development processes, such as synchronize and stabilize [Cus99] and extreme programming [Bec99], evolved to meet the demand for constructing large, complex feature-rich software products in a flexible manner. While such approaches emphasize efficient adaptability to incorporating new technologies, shifting priorities, and competition-driven features, these benefits come at the expense of discipline (e.g., formal design, code review, and complete testing) and schedule. The goal of producing a shippable product can take precedence over the elimination of known errors. While most errors are benign with respect to security, an unresolved implementation error may create a serious security vulnerability. Efforts are underway in industry, academia, and government to improve the quality of software, such as Microsoft's Secure Development Lifecycle [SDL].

3.1.4 Quality of Software Applications

Application development suffers from many of the same problems that affect software products: emphasizing functionality over security, speedy deployment over comprehensive testing, and technology for technology's sake. In striving to offer greater functionality and flexibility, software developers continue to obscure the distinctions between code and data. Furthermore, the prevalence of unintentional implementation errors in software applications that process electronic documents continues to plague active content technology. Since commercial software products underpin most application development, the overall effect of quality problems can be compounded. Even if an application design is correct and secure, the implementation may unintentionally contain serious vulnerabilities that can be exploited by malicious code conveyed in an active content document. An attacker needs only to learn what software the target is using, find an appropriate exploit, and entice the target to download the document.

3.1.5 Complexity of Software

The trend in application software development is to add more features and greater complexity to products. Greater complexity requires more code and more interaction among components, resulting in greater difficulty in discerning the security implications of those interactions, as well as the potential for more implementation errors. This trend, combined with the competitive pressures facing manufacturers to be first to the market, the technical and cost barriers to extensive testing, and a marketplace that chooses functionality over security, assures attackers of continual opportunities in the future.

Web content in particular has become increasingly complex. Many popular Web browsers fail to follow the numerous applicable standards the same way, as demonstrated by the Acid2 test provided by the Web Standards Project (WaSP).[4] The Acid2 test is a single page that tests browser compatibility against HTML4, CSS1, Portable Network Graphics (PNG), and Data URLs. The differences in browser implementations increase the complexity of Web content by requiring developers to construct content that compensates for individual browser capabilities rather than relying on a single code base.

3.1.6 Configuration of Software

Understanding a system's security posture and correctly setting its configuration is an unrealistic expectation for the general population. The usability of most user interfaces for security configurations is low. Yet, users are increasingly relied upon to exercise such skills, particularly with their own Web browsers and desktop software configuration. Even knowledgeable enterprise system administrators are faced with a similar challenge: confronted with an array of security solutions, including those involving company proprietary and incompatible mechanisms, they must oversee a fragile patchwork of software products and devices that demand constant oversight. Additionally, manufacturers use a variety of mechanisms for patch distribution. Patches may also introduce defects into the system—for example, a patch might break other applications by modifying the functionality of a library on which those applications depend. As such, administrators should test each patch before applying it, increasing the window of exposure for systems on their network.

3.1.7 Privacy Practices of Industry

Organizations are increasingly using their Internet offerings to collect information on individuals, both directly (e.g., during credit card purchases and free service subscriptions) or indirectly (e.g., via persistent cookies, Web bugs, and spyware). The latter can expose sensitive data that is stored at the client and identifiable with the user. These actions exacerbate the aforementioned security problems, since successful attacks launched against servers can also affect the privacy of individuals whose information resides there.

---

[4]   More information about WaSP is available at http://www.webstandards.org/.

3.1.8 Limits of Safeguards

Completely defending against all attacks in an open network such as the Internet is not possible. At minimum, the possibility exists for the occurrence of remotely launched denial of service attacks, which consume resources and deny the processing of legitimate requests by flooding the target with bogus requests. Distributed denial of service attacks, launched from a botnet under the control of a single attacker, demonstrate both the ease in which the capacity of any Web site can be overwhelmed and the value of having complete site redundancy for critical services.

3.2 Basic Threat Model

Active content operates at the application layer. Active content technologies allow code, often in the form of a script, macro, or other mobile code representation, to execute when the document is rendered. HTML and other related markup language documents, whether delivered via HTTP or another means, provide rich mechanisms for conveying executable content. Nevertheless, it is important to note that many other types of document formats, although not as rich in mechanisms or not conveyed through the same means, have similar potential.

A more general view of the production and handling of active content is the producer-consumer model illustrated in Figure 3-1, where a producer composes an electronic document containing some form of executable code in addition to text, graphic images, audio, and video content. A producer could range from a user creating macros for a word processing document to a Web server dynamically generating Web pages. By some means, the document is transferred to a consumer who renders it with an application, such as a word processor or Web browser. The execution environments provided for nearly all active content technologies can impose a level of policy restrictions, from limiting the code's access to computational resources during a rendition of the document to only executing code from trusted producers.

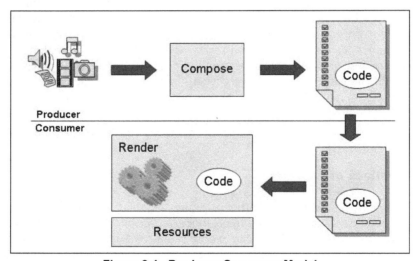

Figure 3-1. Producer-Consumer Model

While any means used to compose, deliver, and render active content automatically is a concern, this guide focuses on the Web, because the associated technologies are designed and implemented to work together seamlessly under this framework, with a user often unaware of the security implications. Figure 3-2 illustrates a simplified Web-based transaction supported by HTTP's client-server architecture. HTTP enables any content to be conveyed from one platform (i.e., a Web server) to another (i.e., a client browser) where it is rendered automatically, executing active content as required. As depicted in the figure, not only can the server impact the browser by supplying it code to execute, but the reverse is also true: input from the browser can influence the execution at the server. As discussed in Section 2, the process of rendering the active content is more involved than what is illustrated in Figure 3-2. Nevertheless, conceptually the depiction is accurate; the supplier of the code and the operator of the execution environment can be from different domains, posing a security risk for each side.

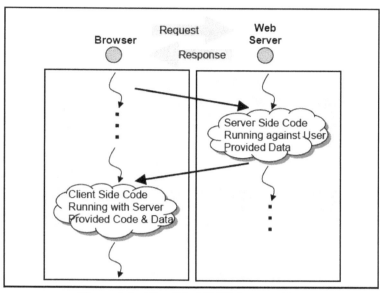

Figure 3-2. Simplified HTTP Transaction

Although Web transactions can be visualized as simple HTTP interchanges between a browser and a Web server, they often are more complex, involving other computer platforms. For example, the Web server may rely on a database server or other online repository or computational engine to fulfill requests it receives. HTTP also accommodates redirection by allowing a Web server to provide referrals to other servers that host requested resources. The redirected Web server could in turn provide further redirection to other servers, if needed. Figure 3-3 gives a more complete picture of some of the other entities that could be involved in Web transactions.

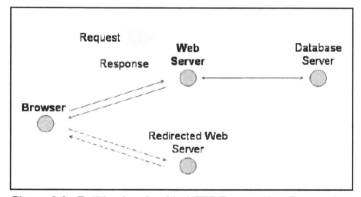

Figure 3-3. Entities Involved in HTTP Transaction Processing

Soon after early forms of active content began to appear on Web sites, some of the fundamental security concerns associated with the design of the Web were recognized [Coh95]:

■ **Distributed untrusted computation.** "As a basic premise, the Web provides a means for information provided by arbitrary servers at unknown locations operated by unknown organizations to be interpreted by any of a large number of different browsers at unknown locations operated by unknown organizations. The idea of interpreting unknown information from unknown sources seems inherently risky."

■ **Remote execution of untrusted software.** "Many Web extensions are designed to provide added function making the Web more than just a massive uncontrolled distributed database. These extensions, such as PostScript, Java, and MIME essentially allow for remote execution of untrusted software. For the browser, the risk is that the computer running the browser will be taken over, while for a server, the same risk extends to the server and any subsequent browsers that get information from that server once it is attacked."

■ **Remote interpretation of unstructured and unverified content.** "In essence, most browsers and servers assume that the incoming information follows the HTTP protocol, but there is inadequate enforcement of this by servers and browsers. The result is that any incoming information might not conform, might be interpreted using an undefined method (corresponding to a don't care condition in the interpreter), and might result in arbitrary undesirable side effects."

Since then, mobile code has become increasingly popular on the Web. Most modern Web browsers execute JavaScript by default. Similarly, Web browsers provide extension capabilities to support third-party mobile code execution environments through ActiveX or browser plug-ins. For example, Sun provides a Java plug-in, while Adobe provides Flash and PDF plug-ins.

Two primary threats associated with mobile code have been noted: malicious logic and malicious hosts [Zac03]. Malicious logic executing as mobile code attempts to compromise the host computer system in some manner through the interfaces available. Similarly, a malicious host computer system may attempt to compromise the mobile code, affecting the Web transaction as a whole, by performing one of the following actions:

■ **Inspection.** A malicious host may gain insight into the Web site as a whole by decomposing the mobile code used.

■ **Modification.** A malicious host may modify the actions performed by the mobile code in an attempt to compromise the Web site or perform an unexpected action.

■ **Replay.** A host may attempt to run the mobile code one or more times without requesting it from the producer.

■ **Denial of service.** A host may not run the mobile code at all, which may adversely affect any associated Web transactions.

Coupled with the concerns associated with the Web, the prevalence of mobile code has exacerbated the threats facing computer systems on the Web. As such, it is important to ensure proper protections and mitigations are in place, as discussed in Section 5.

3.3 Categories of Threats

A number of generic security threats apply to systems on the Internet, for example, unauthorized release of information, modification of information, and denial of service. The Web is subject to these same threats. In addition, the capabilities for supporting active content and mobile code provide new threat opportunities that fall within these general categories. Like any technology, active content can provide a useful capability but can also become a source of vulnerability for an attacker to exploit. Overall, four different classes of attacks against this framework exist: browser-oriented, server-oriented, network-oriented, and user-oriented attacks. While our emphasis is on browser-oriented attacks, the other attack classes are important because they may provide an avenue for launching a browser-oriented attack. Keep in mind that other desktop applications, particularly email clients, often possess browser-like capabilities that are susceptible to browser-oriented attacks. Users may also install unapproved network-enabled applications, such as instant messaging clients, that can serve as a means for delivering active content malware.

3.3.1 Browser-Oriented Attacks

Attacks can be launched against Web browser components and technologies with active content from a Web server. The mobile code paradigm requires a browser to accept and execute code developed elsewhere. The downloaded code containing malware may originate not only from the Web application developer, but also from secondary sources such as banner ads used by many sites to direct one to a product site, or uploaded user content made available through social networking sites [Goo08b, Nad07, Pro08].

Malicious incoming code has two main methods of attack. The first is to gain unauthorized access to computational resources residing at the browser (e.g., security options) or its underlying platform (e.g., system registry). The second is to use its authorized access based on the user's identity in an unexpected and disruptive fashion (e.g., invade privacy or deny service). Because browsers can support multiple associations with different Web servers as separate windowed contexts, the mobile code of one context can also target another context. Unauthorized access may occur simply through a lack of adequate access control mechanisms or weak identification and authentication controls, which allow untrusted code to act or masquerade as a trusted component.

Attackers may take advantage of browser vulnerabilities in mobile code execution environments. Once access is gained, information residing at the platform can be disclosed or altered. Attackers may install spyware, connect the platform to a botnet, or modify the platform's configuration. Depending on the level of access, complete control of the platform may be taken over by the mobile code. Even without gaining unauthorized access to resources, malicious code can deny platform services to other processes by exhausting computational resources, if resource constraints are not established or not set tightly.

3.3.2 Server-Oriented Attacks

Attacks can be launched against Web server components and technologies as the first stage of a larger scheme. For example, a browser or other utility can be used to isolate and capture a response from a server, which may be manipulated and fed back to the server in a subsequent request in an attempt to take advantage of a Web application's failure to sanitize user input. The objective is to induce the server to perform unauthorized commands provided by the browser as user input, which in turn gains an attacker access to sensitive information or control of the server. User-provided input might be passed to an application interface that treats the input as part of a Structured Query Language (SQL) command to retrieve sensitive data such as login information (i.e., SQL injection attack). Attackers may also inject malicious custom code into a Web site's content, and that code is subsequently served to the site's users (i.e., cross-site scripting [XSS] attack).

A compromised server can be used against browsers attempting to interact with it. Subtle changes introduced into the Web server could radically change the server's behavior, turning a trusted entity into a malicious one [Car08]. The reliability of the output supplied (e.g., delivering incorrect results, malware, or referral links to malicious sites) and the confidentiality of any information submitted (e.g., sensitive personal data) would be at risk.

3.3.3 Network-Oriented Attacks

Attacks can be launched against the network infrastructure used to communicate between the browser and server. An attacker can gain information by masquerading as a Web server using a man-in-the-middle attack, whereby requests and responses are conveyed via the imposter as a watchful intermediary. Such a *Web spoofing attack* allows the impostor to shadow not only a single targeted server, but also every subsequent server accessed [Fel97]. Other attack methods lie outside the browser-server framework and involve targeting the communications or the supporting platforms. For example, at a level of protocol below HTTP, an entity may eavesdrop on messages in transit between a browser and server to glean information. Many diagnostic tools, such as packet sniffers, can reconstruct HTTP traffic from captured IP packets. An attacking entity may also intercept messages in transit and modify their contents, substitute other contents, or simply replay the transmission dialogue later in an attempt to disrupt the synchronization or integrity of the information. For example, an attacker may modify the DNS mechanisms used by a computer to direct it to a false Web site. These techniques are often used to perform pharming attacks, where users may divulge sensitive information. Denial of service attacks through available network interfaces are another possibility, as well as exploits involving any existing platform vulnerability.

3.3.4 User-Oriented Attacks

Increasingly, attackers use social engineering combined with other techniques to target Web users. Often, these attacks occur in the form of phishing attacks, where attackers try to trick users into accessing a fake Web site and divulging personal information. In some phishing attacks, users receive a legitimate-looking email asking them to update their information on the company's Web site. Instead of legitimate links, however, the URLs in the email actually point to a rogue Web site.[5] Other phishing attacks are more advanced and take advantage of vulnerabilities in the legitimate Web site's application. For example, a security flaw in the PayPal web site was exploited to steal credit card numbers and other personal information belonging to its users. Visiting users were presented with a message that had been injected into the site that said, "Your account is currently disabled because we think it has been accessed by a third party. You will now be redirected to Resolution Center." and then redirected to the attacker's Web site [Net06].

3.4 Threat Summary

This section discussed the threats facing organizations and individuals due to increasing reliance on mobile code in Web applications. Many of these threats are a result of security issues that were not addressed when Internet protocols were developed. Although these omissions contribute to the threats facing Web users, they are exacerbated by the scale of the Internet, the complexity of software, and the prevalence of mobile code. Many Web interactions rely on mobile code, either running on a Web server or Web browser. As such, Web interactions are susceptible to threats facing mobile code as well. These factors cause organizations to face four classes of attacks: browser-oriented, server-oriented, network-oriented, and user-oriented. Section 5 provides information about mitigating the threats posed by each class of attack.

---

[5] NIST SP 800-45 version 2, *Guidelines on Electronic Mail Security*, contains information on detecting phishing emails. It is available at http://csrc.nist.gov/publications/PubsSPs.html.

4.   Technology Related Risks

Risk is a measure of the likelihood and the consequence of events or acts that could cause a system compromise, including the unauthorized disclosure, destruction, removal, modification, or interruption of system assets [NIST02]. Many computer technologies involve risk, since they can introduce some degree of vulnerability to a system due to flaws or weaknesses in the technologies' design, implementation, or configuration. More generally, a security vulnerability is the absence of or weakness in the security controls for a system that could result in a violation of the system's security policy. While technology-related vulnerabilities are often subtle and do not affect either the overall functionality or performance of a product, they may be discovered and exploited by an attacker. The impact of a vulnerability on an individual or organization is the subject of a risk analysis and can vary widely, depending on such factors as the value of the resource affected or the perceived harm to one's reputation.[6]

To better explain the range of risks associated with active content, some popular active content technologies and their vulnerabilities are described in the remainder of this section. The motivation behind these technologies is to improve functionality and gain flexibility for the user. In a Web application, improvements often involve moving code processing away from the Web server onto the client's Web browser. As pointed out in the previous sections, allowing remote systems to run arbitrary code on a local system poses serious security risks. While most of the technologies to be discussed provide a useful capability, many of them can also be exploited by an attacker.

> **Privacy Risks:** Security does not necessarily imply privacy. One may securely transmit personal or credit card information to a company, but information about who within or outside the company has access to the information is generally unknown. Although privacy breaches directly affect individuals, they can also affect the organizations for which the affected individuals work. For example, the inkling, unsubstantiated or not, that a company's CEO is suffering from a serious illness can cause its stock value to plummet.
>
> Some organizations link records from different sources to target marketing efforts and to assess risks. When taken collectively, such information constitutes an electronic dossier on an individual, which in the wrong hands can cause harm, even if it is not completely accurate. No one can learn the full extent of the information kept on them by various organizations, much less verify accuracy or control access. Much of the information collected over the Internet occurs in the background, without the individual's knowledge or consent. For example, many organizations have distributed free plug-ins or other software containing *spyware* – functionality that, once installed, periodically sends reports back to the company about its use and its environment.
>
> Besides spyware, Web site developers have a myriad of tools at their disposal to collect personal information. They include tracking site use by storing persistent information known as *cookies* via a user's browser; embedding invisible single-pixel images within HTML called *Web bugs* that serve as a signal of page access; and invoking the communication capabilities of downloaded scripts and program components.

---

[6]   For more information on risk analysis for IT systems, see NIST SP 800-30 at http://csrc.nist.gov/publications/PubsSPs.html.

Servers routinely log information that identifies users indirectly by recording client host names and even, when available, user names, and gives information about the request. Users may not be aware that such logs are being collected and most likely have no idea how that information is used, how long it is retained or whether it is shared with third parties. There are few legal rules or ethical guidelines in many countries governing the disposition of log information, such as the sale to other organizations where they may be combined with other databases (e.g., online address listings) to infer further information.

4.1 Client-Side Technologies

Two main factors should be considered when attempting to gauge the risk involved with active content technologies on the client side: the capabilities of the programming language, and the breadth and strength of controls in place within the execution environment to enforce policy. Different technologies offer a distinctive range of functionality regarding the granularity and types of actions that can be performed on computational resources, such as windows, files, or network ports. Similarly, security policy controls may provide different levels of granularity, enforced at different points of time (e.g., vetting the code before it executes versus restricting its activities as it runs), resulting in varied degrees of effectiveness. For instance, JavaScript implemented within a browser environment normally prevents a downloaded script from reading or writing files by making file objects unavailable. In contrast, an ActiveX control, once accepted, can have complete reign over the entire file system. Determining the acceptable level of risk may involve other factors, such as the maturity of the technology, the scope of its intended use, the experience of the organization with the technology, and other controls the organization has in place.

4.1.1 PostScript

One of the earliest examples of active content is PostScript document representation [Ado99], still in use today. PostScript is a page description language from Adobe that is a de facto standard in commercial typesetting and printing houses. PostScript commands are language statements in ASCII text that are translated into the printer's machine language by a PostScript interpreter built into the printer. PostScript can also be interpreted by software on most computer platforms and drawn on to computer screens or an attached drawing device. The interpreter uses scalable fonts, eliminating the need to store a variety of font sizes.

A PostScript file contains a document description, which is specified in the PostScript page description language. The language is a powerful interpreted language, comparable to many programming languages. Thus, PostScript documents inherently entail active content. For example, the language defines primitives for file manipulation, which can be used in a PostScript document to modify arbitrary files when the document is displayed or printed. Unfortunately, the operations can be abused by intentionally embedding malicious file commands within an otherwise harmless image, so that in displaying the image the interpreter also causes damage.

An early exploit of PostScript technology involved the language's ability to set a password held by the interpreter. In some hardware implementations of the language interpreter, if the password were set, it remained in non-volatile memory and prevented subsequent documents from being printed unless they contained the same password. An attacker sending a password-setting document could disable the printer in this way, requiring hardware replacement to rectify the situation [Cle90, Spe90]. Some PostScript interpreters can be set to disable potentially harmful primitives. For example, ghostscript, a well-known PostScript interpreter, recognizes the command-line option "-dSAFER" that disables file operations, which could be abused to cause damage. One drawback is that applying such safeguards can also inhibit useful functions. This dilemma is a recurring theme with active content.

4.1.2 Portable Document Format (PDF)

Portable Document Format (PDF) [Ado07b] is a page description language from Adobe for specifying the appearance of pages containing text, graphics, and images, using the same high-level, device-independent imaging model employed by PostScript. Unlike PostScript, PDF is not a full-scale programming language and does not include language features such as procedures, variables, and control constructs. A PDF reader, which is used to view or print PDF files, can be installed as either a plug-in or a helper application for a browser. Other full-featured tools exist to generate and manipulate, as well as view and print, PDF files.

A PDF document can be regarded as a hierarchy of objects. For example, a page object, which includes references to the page's contents (i.e., a content stream), other attributes such as its thumbnail image, and any associated annotations, represents each page of the document. A content stream, in turn, is an object whose data consists of a sequence of instructions that describe the graphical elements to be rendered on a page, which are also represented as PDF objects using the same object syntax as the rest of the PDF document. Whereas the document as a whole is a static, random-access data structure, the objects in the content stream are intended to be interpreted and acted upon sequentially.

Because of the object orientation and limited image-rendering operators, PDF is generally considered a benign format for use with a capability-limited content reader or viewer, such as the widely used Adobe Acrobat Reader. However, full-featured PDF tools, such as Adobe Acrobat, may be more susceptible to attack by virtue of their extended functionality. In the past, a demonstration showed that while the format itself may be benign, a PDF file could bear malicious code as an embedded file attachment [Fis01]. When the contaminated PDF file is opened for the demonstration, a game is launched that prompts the user to click on a moving image of a peach. The occurrence of that event, in turn, causes the execution of an embedded VBScript file, which attempts to mail out the PDF file to others using Microsoft Outlook.

Note that even content readers are not completely immune from problems. From time-to-time, vulnerabilities have occurred in the implementation of Acrobat Reader that could be exploited with carefully constructed content. For example, Adobe released a patch to the Acrobat Reader 8 browser plug-in that eliminates a cross-site scripting vulnerability [Ado07a]. An attacker could exploit the vulnerability by appending Javascript to a PDF URL that would cause any version of the reader to execute arbitrary JavaScript code when the file was rendered. This example illustrates how even relatively benign content can affect document rendering software having implementation errors.

PDF does incorporate two distinct security features that can be applied to any conforming document, individually or together. The document can be digitally sealed through a signed document digest, a biometric signature, or other means to certify its authenticity and protect against tampering. The document can also be encrypted so that only authorized users can view or operate on its contents.

4.1.3 Java

Java is a full-featured, object-oriented programming language compiled into platform-independent byte code executed by an interpreter called the Java Virtual Machine (JVM). The resulting byte code can be executed where compiled or transferred to another Java-enabled platform. The Java programming language and runtime environment [Gon98, Gos96] enforce security primarily through the Java security manager, which monitors running Java applications and verifies that they are following a specified policy. The security manager allows Java to follow a sandbox security model, isolating memory and method access and maintaining mutually exclusive execution domains. In Java code, such as an applet, the sandbox is an instance of the Java security manager configured to prevent the applet from performing unauthorized operations. The Java security manager can limit a variety of activities, such as inspecting or changing files on a client file system, using network connections, or even restricting what class libraries the code may access. The Java security manager is flexible and can be configured for any application, providing additional security protections beyond those provided by the OS.

Security is enforced through a variety of mechanisms. Static type checking in the form of byte code verification is used to check aspects of the safety of downloaded code. Some dynamic checking is also performed during runtime. A distinct name space is maintained for distinct packages or modules, and linking of references between packages is restricted to public methods. A security manager mediates all accesses to system resources, serving in effect as a reference monitor. Permissions can be assigned based on the source of the code (where it came from), the author of the code (who developed it), or a specific package name, which restricts the access of the code to computational resources. In addition, Java inherently supports code mobility, dynamic code downloading, digitally signed code, remote method invocation, object serialization, and platform heterogeneity.

Web browsers can download Java byte code from Web sites and run it with restricted privileges as Java applets. Many services offered by various popular Web sites require the user to have a Java-enabled browser. When the Web browser sees references to Java code, it loads the code and then processes it using the built-in JVM with strict permissions enforced by the Java security manager.

Hostile applets still pose security threats even while executing within the sandbox. A hostile applet can consume or exploit system resources inappropriately or cause a user to perform an undesired or unwanted action. Examples of hostile applet exploits are denial of service, mail forging, invasion of privacy (e.g., exporting of identity, email address, and platform information), and installing backdoors to the system. The Java security model is rather complex and can be difficult to understand and manage, which can increase risk. Moreover, implementation bugs have also been found that allow security mechanisms to be bypassed [Sun07]. Finally, signed Java applets are often run without restrictions; attackers able to coerce users into loading a hostile signed applet will be able to bypass many of Java's security mechanisms.

4.1.4   JavaScript, VBScript, and AJAX

JavaScript is a general-purpose scripting language available in most Web browsers. It can be embedded within standard Web pages to create interactive documents. Each JavaScript interpreter supplies the needed objects to control the execution environment, and because of differences the functionality can vary considerably. Within the context of a Web browser, the language is powerful, allowing prepared scripts to modify the Web page and perform calculations on the client side, improving perceived performance and potentially reducing the load on the server. Within a browser context, JavaScript does not have methods for directly accessing a client file system or for directly opening connections to other computers besides the host that provided the content source. Moreover, the browser normally confines a script's execution to the page in which it was downloaded.

The name JavaScript is a misnomer since the language has little relationship to Java technology and arose independently from it. Netscape developed JavaScript for its Navigator browser, and eventually JScript, a variation of JavaScript, appeared in Microsoft's Internet Explorer. Standardizing the core language and facilities of JavaScript and JScript resulted in the ECMAScript Language Specification [ECMA99], which most modern Web browsers support. Design and implementation bugs have been discovered in the commercial scripting products provided with many browsers, including those from Microsoft, Apple, Mozilla, and Opera.

Visual Basic Script (VBScript) is a programming language developed by Microsoft for creating scripts that can be embedded in Web pages for viewing with the Internet Explorer browser. Alternative browsers do not support VBScript. Like JavaScript, VBScript is an interpreted language able to process client-side scripts. VBScript is a subset of the widely used Microsoft Visual Basic programming language and works with Microsoft ActiveX controls. The language is similar to JavaScript and poses similar risks.

In theory, confining a scripting language to the boundaries of a Web browser should provide a relatively secure environment. In practice, this has not been the case. Many browser-based attacks stem from the use of a scripting language in combination with a security vulnerability. The main sources of problems have been twofold: the prevalence of implementation flaws in the execution environment and the close binding of the browser to related functionality such as an email client. Past exploits include sending a user's URL history list to a remote site, and using the mail address of the user to forge email. The increasing use of client scripting technologies at Web sites has opened new avenues for exploits.

JavaScript is one of the main components of AJAX, a collection of technologies that allows Web developers to improve the user interaction and response times for rendering Web content [OAA07]. A second key component is a new browser API that enables JavaScript and other downloaded active content to issue requests to a Web server to convey XML or other well-formatted data. With this API, JavaScript code can communicate with a Web server whenever needed and modify the contents of the Web browser's page selectively as responses are received, instead of waiting for the Web server to respond with an entire page of markup for each request issued. Since only the required data needs to be transmitted, the total amount exchanged with the Web server is reduced. AJAX allows Web content to behave more like traditional applications, but with increased complexity, which also increases the attack surface of a Web application. Security concerns raised about AJAX include the following [SPI06]:

■ AJAX increases the number of points where a client interacts with the application.

■ AJAX may reveal details of internal functions within the Web application.

■ Some AJAX endpoints may not require authentication, relying instead on the current state of the application.

While AJAX is more of a perspective on the architecture of web applications that employ certain technologies, numerous AJAX frameworks also exist that provide developers with JavaScript functions to send requests and process them at the server. A framework usually includes an AJAX engine that is downloaded to the browser to render the user interface and communicate with the server. Selecting a suitable AJAX framework requires ensuring that the security requirements of the application can be satisfied through the architecture provided.

4.1.5 ActiveX

ActiveX is a set of technologies from Microsoft that provides tools for linking desktop applications to the Web. ActiveX controls are reusable component program objects that can be attached to email or downloaded from a Web site. Many ActiveX controls come preinstalled on Windows OSs. Web pages invoke ActiveX controls using a scripting language or via a HTML OBJECT tag. It is possible to specify a URL where the control may be obtained if it is not installed locally. Unlike Java, which is a platform-independent programming language, ActiveX controls are distributed as executable binaries tailored for a Windows operating environment. Web users normally encounter ActiveX technology in one of the following forms:

■ ActiveX controls, formerly known as Object Linking and Embedding (OLE) controls, are components (or objects) of prepackaged functionality that can be inserted into a Web page or other application for reuse. ActiveX controls are included with Microsoft Internet Explorer to allow Web pages to be enhanced with formatting, special effects, or animation.

■ ActiveX documents allow an ActiveX-enabled Web browser to open an application, with the application's own toolbars and menus available, and serve as its container. This allows non-HTML native-formatted files, such as Microsoft Excel, Microsoft Word, or PDF files, to be opened and manipulated when encountered by the browser.

■ ActiveX scripting refers to enhancements to VBScript and JavaScript to interact with ActiveX controls. ActiveX scripting can be used to integrate the behavior of several ActiveX controls or Java applications from the Web browser or server, extending their functionality.

The ActiveX security model is considerably different from the Java sandbox model [Ste02]. The Java model is designed to restrict the permissions of applets to a set of safe actions based on the source or author of the code via the Java security manager. Instead, ActiveX controls are digitally signed by their author under a technology scheme called *Authenticode*. The digital signatures are verified using identity certificates issued by a trusted certificate authority to an ActiveX software publisher. For an ActiveX publisher's certificate to be granted, the software publisher must pledge that no harmful code will be knowingly distributed under this scheme. The Authenticode security model is designed to ensure that ActiveX controls cannot be distributed anonymously and that tampering with the controls can be detected, but it imposes few restrictions on the actions controls can take once they are executing.

Recent versions of Internet Explorer allow the user to categorize ActiveX controls depending on whether they are downloaded from a site on the Internet, a site on the local intranet, or a site identified as being either trusted or untrusted by the user. These site categories are known as security zones. Each zone can be configured to disable or enable the automatic loading of different classes of ActiveX controls (e.g., signed versus unsigned) from a site in the zone, or to prompt the user for a decision before downloading them.

When prompting the user, the browser presents a dialog box warning that downloading the control may not be safe. The user can choose to abort the transfer or, if the the source is believed to be trustworthy or low-risk, continue it. Users may not be aware of the security implications of their decisions, which can have serious repercussions. Even when the user is well informed, attackers may trick the user into approving the transfer. In the past, attackers have exploited implementation flaws to cover the user dialogue window with another that displays an unobtrusive message such as "Do you want to continue?" while exposing the positive indication button needed to launch active content.

Like any other application that supports mobile code, ActiveX-enabled browsers provide a potential vehicle for malicious code delivery. If a user decides to download an ActiveX control from a malicious Web site, the control is automatically executed without the victim having to take any further action. Instead of developing malicious controls to propagate, some attackers have successfully exploited flaws in ActiveX controls that have been distributed by trusted publishers [Kei08]. This sort of attack may be the most dangerous, since the user may assume that a control is safe due to its source and have no concerns about security or privacy when it executes.

4.1.6 Desktop Application Macros

Developers of popular spreadsheet, word processing, and other desktop applications included macro features to allow users to automate and customize repetitive tasks. A macro, in its simplest form, is a series of menu selections, keystrokes, and commands recorded and assigned a name or key combination. When the macro name is called or the macro key combination is pressed, the steps in the macro are executed from beginning to end. Macros are used to shorten long menu sequences as well as to create programs within an application. More complex macro languages often include programming controls (such as *if*, *else*, or *while* statements) and language features that make them comparable to a scripting language. A virus can be written as a macro stored in a spreadsheet or a word processing document. When the document is opened for viewing or use, the macro will be executed and the virus activated. It may also attach itself to subsequent documents that are saved with the application. For these reasons, under normal circumstances desktop applications should not be configured to open automatically for another desktop application, such as a browser or email client, that receives untrusted content.

The Melissa virus illustrates the risk involved [Sha99]. A Microsoft Word document containing a malicious Visual Basic for Applications (VBA) macro propagated itself through the Internet by sending the host document as an email attachment addressed to contacts found in the previous victim's address book. A contact opening the attachment permitted the macro to execute and the virus to take hold. As with many macro languages, VBA is an integral part of Microsoft Office applications, included as a means for developers to build custom solutions within that environment. VBA is a superset of VBScript and offers the same automation and customization capabilities, but within the context of a desktop application.

The newer generation of email applications, including the ones built into Web browsers, support HTML content, MIME attachments and—potentially, via AJAX, JavaScript. Since active content provides many avenues for exploits, such mail content should be opened only after consideration of the inherent risks. These risks exist in part because of the dual roles for which HTML is being used. On the one hand, HTML is surpassing plain, non-tagged ASCII as a common means for composing and exchanging documents. On the other hand, HTML is also being used as an environment to house such scripting languages, Java applets, and ActiveX components. By combining the flexibility to send and receive HTML content with its ability to embody scripts and other forms of programs that have full access to memory and files, the potential for abuse increases.

4.1.7 Plug-ins and Extensions

Plug-ins and extensions are native code modules or scripts that work in conjunction with software applications to enhance their capabilities. Plug-ins are often added to Web browsers to enable them to support new types of content (e.g. additional audio or video formats), while extensions typically add new functionality to the browser (e.g., improved bookmarking). Plug-ins and extensions have also been devised for email clients and other desktop software. They can be downloaded from either the browser manufacturer's site or a third-party site. Browsers typically prompt the user to download a new plug-in when a document requires functionality beyond the browser's current capabilities. Although plug-ins and extensions allow browsers to support new types of content and functionality, they are not active content in and of themselves, but simply executables that enable active content technologies. Windows Media Player, RealPlayer, QuickTime, ShockWave, and Flash are all examples of plug-ins that allow browsers to support new content types, such as audio, video, and interactive animation. Extensions are usually browser-specific, offering a variety of functionality from FTP clients to automatic form fill-out.

Thus, there are two security concerns with plug-ins and extensions: the behavior of active content processed by an installed plug-in, and the behavior of the plug-in executables themselves once they are downloaded and installed. Plug-ins and extensions can bypass a browser's underlying security model. For instance, the ShockWave plug-in from Adobe provides the ability to render multimedia presentations (created in a compatible format) as they are downloaded. By design, Shockwave content supports the Lingo interpretative language as an aid to presentation development. Early versions of Lingo allowed the author to make local system calls based on the platform executing the content, potentially allowing malicious code to be downloaded as part of the presentation. Another example is the Firefox browser extension called GreaseMonkey that allows users to install scripts to make dynamic changes to HTML

Web pages as they are downloaded, often by augmenting their functionality through other Web resources. To accomplish its tasks, it provides a means to bypass the same origin policy of the browser and interact with any domain, which could be exploited by a malicious Web site.

From a security standpoint, plug-ins are executable code, and precautions should be exercised in obtaining and installing them, as with any other software application. Downloading plug-ins directly from a reputable manufacturer is normally less risky than downloading them from other sources, but even in the first case, it is difficult for the user to be aware of the security implications. In the past, unwanted side effects such as changes to browser security settings and tracking of a user's content preferences, albeit well intentioned, have occurred. Plug-ins designed to animate cursors or hyperlinks have also been designed to track user preferences and viewing habits across a particular Web site more accurately. Although these capabilities may improve the user's experience with a particular Web site, the privacy and security implications are often not readily disclosed [Mar00]. Even if the site has a valid identity certificate associated with the signed downloaded code, that only tells the user that the manufacturer of the code has been verified by a certificate authority, not whether the code obtained from them will behave non-maliciously or correctly. Users of plug-ins should be cautioned to read the fine print before agreeing to download executables and take adequate measures to backup the system in the event of problems.

4.2   Server-Side Technologies

Unlike the technologies described above, Web applications, which rely on CGI or other server-side content-generating components, fall on the producer side of the producer-consumer model. Through such components, Web applications can be written in most programming languages to run on a Web server. More often than not, a server-side scripting language or framework such as Perl, .NET, or Java Enterprise Edition (Java EE) is used for this purpose, because of its flexibility, compactness, and robustness. If these programs are not prepared carefully, attackers can find and exercise flaws in the code to compromise the Web server. A compromised Web server may eventually be used to deliver malicious active content to Web browsers visiting the site. Server scripts and code modules should be written with security in mind and, for example, should not run arbitrary commands on a system or launch insecure programs. Even content files generated with authoring tools may contain vulnerabilities that can be exploited [CERT08, Goo08a]. An attacker can find flaws through trial and error and does not necessarily need the source code or a content generating tool to uncover vulnerabilities.

Three general areas exist where server applications can introduce security vulnerabilities at the server:

■ They may intentionally or unintentionally leak information about the host system that can aid an attacker, for example, by allowing access to information outside the areas designated for Web use.

■ When processing user-provided input, such as the contents of a form, URL parameters, or a search query, they may be able to be tricked into executing arbitrary commands supplied in the input stream.

■ When returning user-provided content, such as an email or uploaded video, they may deliver malicious content constructed by attackers for execution in other users' Web browsers.

The three areas of vulnerability mentioned potentially affect all Web servers. Active content generating technologies used at the server are frequently the source of these vulnerabilities. CGI has gained particular notoriety over the years, because it was an early and well-supported standard. However, the same types of vulnerabilities exist when applying similar Web development technologies at the server. An in-depth discussion on this matter can be found in NIST SP 800-44 Version 2, *Guidelines on Securing Public Web Servers* [NIST07].

The line between Web applications and locally installed applications has blurred over time to the point where a number of Web application providers offer Web versions of common desktop productivity tools, including word processors, spreadsheets, and calendars. In fact, a number of organizations are adopting these Web-based applications in place of standalone applications [Bee07]. As such, these Web applications may need to support the ability to store and process mobile code associated with office documents (or any user-generated files), opening up Web applications to many of the risks discussed earlier in this section.

4.2.1 Server Side Includes

Server Side Includes (SSI) is a limited server-side scripting language supported by most Web servers. SSI provides a set of dynamic features, such as including the current time or the last modification date of the HTML file, as an alternative to using a CGI program to perform the function. When the browser requests a document with a special file type, such as *.shtml*, it triggers the server to treat the document as a template, reading and parsing the entire document before sending the results back to the client (Web browser). SSI commands are embedded within HTML comments (e.g., <!--#include file="standard.html" -->). As the server reads the template file, it searches for HTML comments containing embedded SSI commands. When it finds one, the server replaces that part of the original HTML text with the output of the command. For example, the SSI command given above (i.e., #include file) replaces the entire SSI comment with the contents of another HTML file. This allows the display of an organization logo or other static information prepared in another file to occur in a uniform way across all organization Web pages. A subset of the directives available allows the server to execute arbitrary system commands and CGI scripts, which may produce unwanted results. SSI is susceptible to command injection attacks, which involve an attacker providing malicious code that is processed and executed by the Web server. This allows the attacker to run arbitrary system commands using the privileges of the Web server.

4.2.2 Java Enterprise Edition (EE)

Java Enterprise Edition (EE) is based on Java technology and provides a comprehensive means to develop applications on the server based largely on modular components. A type of server-side applet called a servlet is used to provide dynamic content. The Web server first determines whether the browser's request requires a static HTML page or dynamically generated information from a servlet or a Java Server Page (JSP). If a servlet is required, the Web server locates or instantiates a servlet object corresponding to the request, then invokes it to obtain the needed results. If a JSP is required, Java EE compiles the JSP into a servlet, then instantiates and invokes the servlet to obtain a response. If a static HTML page is requested, the HTML content is returned as with a traditional Web server.

The Java EE server typically populates itself with the servlet objects that remain inactive until invoked. This results in little or no startup overhead when processing servlet objects. Java EE can also run separately from a standalone Web server, allowing one host to handle the brunt of HTTP traffic while another handles the servlets. By relying on Java portability and observing a common API, servlet objects can run in nearly any server environment. Servlets allow developers to take advantage of an object-oriented environment on the Web server, which is flexible and extendible. Moreover, untrusted servlet objects can be executed in a secure area via the Java security manager, with the dynamically generated information being passed from the secure area into the remaining server environment.

4.2.3 ASP.NET

Microsoft's Active Server Pages (ASP).NET is a server-side scripting technology from Microsoft that can be used to create dynamic and interactive Web applications. An ASP page is essentially a template that contains server-side scripts which are executed when a browser requests a *.asp* resource from the Web server. The Web server processes the requested page and executes any script commands encountered before sending a generated HTML page to the user's browser.

Both C# and VBScript are natively supported as ASP.NET scripting languages, but other languages can be accommodated through the Common Language Runtime (CLR), which provides common services such as cross-language integration, cross-language exception handling, and security. ASP.NET scripting engines are available for the PERL, REXX, and Python languages from various sources. Scripting capabilities can also be extended through the use of ActiveX objects, which can be developed in a variety of languages, including Visual Basic, C++, Cobol, and Java. A script that invokes an ActiveX object causes the object to be created and supplies any needed input parameters. While Microsoft's .NET platform was originally limited to its Windows OS, Novell sponsors the Mono project, which implements the ECMA standards for C# and CLR on UNIX-like OSs.[7]

As with Java, code written in .NET can be downloaded and run from untrusted sources. To alleviate this problem, Microsoft has integrated code access security into the .NET Framework. Code access security provides various levels of trust for code based on where the code originates and allows individual users to specify what permissions will be given to an application. Because code access security is part of the .NET Framework, all applications that access the .NET Framework can be subject to code access security. Because policies are defined on a per machine basis, libraries are provided that allow applications to determine whether the application has a particular permission before performing a potentially restricted act—allowing .NET applications to alter their behavior rather than simply generate a security exception. Nevertheless, like Java, implementation bugs have been found in .NET that may allow attackers to bypass security mechanisms [MS07].

4.2.4   C# and Visual Basic .NET (VB.NET)

C# (pronounced C sharp) is a strongly typed, object-oriented programming language that enables programmers to build applications for the Microsoft .NET platform. C# borrows most of its operators, keywords, and statements from C++ and is intended to be used in programming both hosted and embedded systems. C# is normally compiled into Microsoft Intermediate Language (MSIL) byte codes and then just-in-time compiled into native code during execution, but also can be compiled directly into native code. The language and security features (through code access security) are similar to Java's and pose similar risks.

VB.NET was released alongside of C# as a successor to the legacy Visual Basic language. While the VB.NET syntax is similar to the original Visual Basic language, VB.NET provides a fully object-oriented language in place of the component object model (COM)-based language of Visual Basic. While Visual Basic has some security concerns, VB.NET's support of garbage collection, object-oriented design, code access security, and the .NET framework make VB.NET similar to C#. Through the .NET framework and the CLR, VB.NET has access to .NET's security libraries and is protected by code access security.

4.2.5   PHP Hypertext Preprocessor (PHP)

PHP is a scripting language used to create dynamic Web pages. With a syntax borrowed from the C, Java, and Perl programming languages, PHP code is embedded within HTML pages for server-side execution. PHP is commonly used to extract data from a database and present it on a Web page. Most major Windows and Unix Web servers support the language, and it is widely used with the mySQL database. PHP provides a number of options that simplify development. Nevertheless, it is a rich, powerful scripting environment with subtle processing implications, and some options can make it more

---

[7]   More information about the Mono project is available at http://www.mono-project.com/.

difficult for novices to develop secure programs. For example, the register_globals option, used to convert all input parameters into PHP variables, may allow user input to override values in the PHP script, if not handled appropriately [Clo01].

4.3   Risk Summary

This section presented the technology-based risks associated with active content and mobile code. Any technology that allows untrusted code to execute on a system may introduce risks. In particular, all software contains defects, some of which may be exploitable vulnerabilities—potentially allowing an attacker to run arbitrary code on the machine. As such, there are two main factors to consider when determining the risk associated with active content: the capabilities of the programming language and the security controls provided by the execution environment. Nevertheless, in many situations, it may be necessary to deploy an active content technology regardless of the risk determination, such as when a critical system requires JavaScript or PDF support, taking appropriate caution.

As both the consumer and producer sides of the Web model increasingly support and require active content, it becomes ever more important for organizations to be aware of and address the risks they may be facing. The next section, Section 5, covers some of the safeguards that can be put in place to mitigate many of these risks.

5. Safeguards

Safeguards are approved security measures taken to prevent or reduce the risk of system compromise. To protect computational resources from attack, appropriate safeguards must be in place. To mitigate the risks in using active content, two main approaches can be followed: avoidance – staying completely clear of known and potential vulnerabilities, and risk mitigation – applying measures to limit the potential loss due to exposure. These approaches can be realized through the application of appropriate management, operational, and technical controls as safeguards.

5.1 Management and Operational Safeguards

Common management and operational controls used to safeguard systems against other security threats also apply to active content. The following subsections highlight some of the more useful safeguards that can be applied.

5.1.1 Security Policy

A security policy is the set of rules, principles, and practices that determine how an organization implements its security. A policy reflects an organization's view on required safeguards, based on a consideration of its assets, the impact of loss or compromise, and the threat environment. Information security in any organization is largely dependent on the quality of the security policy and the processes that the organization imposes on itself for implementation, awareness, and enforcement. No amount of technology can overcome a poorly planned or nonexistent security policy. If the policy is not stated clearly and consistently, and not made known and enforced throughout an organization, it creates a situation ripe for exploitation.

Having or establishing an organizational security policy is an important first step in applying safeguards for active content. For example, an Internet security policy can address enabling Java, JavaScript, or ActiveX on an individual user's Web browser in various ways:

- Functionality must be disallowed completely.

- Functionality is allowed, but only from internal organizational servers.

- Functionality is allowed, but only from trusted external servers.

- Functionality is allowed from any server.

One practical difficulty is that functionality often takes precedence over security in product marketing and consumer demand. New technology products may be in use within an organization years before the security policy is written to guide employees. For example, the Department of Defense (DoD) initially formulated its policy and guidance on mobile code technology in 2000. While the policy came years after the respective technology's debut in products, the DoD started to address the problem relatively early, compared to most other organizations.

The DoD policy, which was updated in 2006, delineates three categories of technology based on increasing associated risk [DoD06]. Category 1, the most dangerous, involves technologies having broad functionality and unmediated access to the services and resources of a computing platform. Examples include ActiveX and script languages interpreted at the OS command level. Category 2 involves technologies having full functionality, but mediated or controlled access to the services and resources of a computing platform. Examples are Java mobile code and various scripting languages running within the confines of a browser. Category 3 involves technologies having limited functionality, with no capability for unmediated access to the services and resources of a computing platform. Where possible, the policy distinguishes between signed and unsigned code, favoring the former over the latter.

5.1.2   Risk Analysis and Management

Security involves continually analyzing and managing risks and, as seen in the previous section, active content has its share of risks. Any such analysis should identify vulnerabilities and threats, enumerate potential attacks, assess their likelihood of success, and estimate the potential damage from successful attacks. Risk management is the process of assessing risk, taking steps to reduce risk to an acceptable level, and maintaining that level of risk. Ongoing risk analysis and management is an important organizational activity that is increasingly being mandated by law and regulation.

Security is relative to each organization and needs to be tailored to an organization's specific requirements, budget, and culture. Organizations, much like people, have differing comfort levels on the amount of risk that is reasonable, which may influence this process. Once an assessment is made, safeguards can be put in place against those attacks deemed significantly high by either reducing the likelihood of occurrence or minimizing the consequences of the attack. Different safeguards are employed to meet an organization's specific needs.

The General Accounting Office (GAO) analyzed and summarized information security weaknesses identified in audit reports of Federal agencies [GAO07] issued for fiscal years 2004, 2005 and 2006. They noted that most of the organizations reviewed had not fully implemented agencywide information security programs.

> "An agencywide security program provides a framework and continuing cycle of activity for managing risk, developing security policies, assigning responsibilities, promoting awareness, monitoring the adequacy of the entity's computer-related controls through security tests and evaluations, and implementing remedial actions as appropriate. Without a well-designed program, security controls may be inadequate; responsibilities may be unclear, misunderstood, and improperly implemented; and controls may be inconsistently applied. Such conditions may lead to insufficient protection of sensitive or critical resources… As a result, agencies do not have reasonable assurance that controls are implemented correctly, operating as intended, or producing the desired outcome with respect to meeting the security requirements of the agency. Furthermore, agencies may not be fully aware of the security control weaknesses in their systems, thereby leaving their information and systems vulnerable to attack or compromise. Until agencies effectively and fully implement agencywide information security programs, Federal data and systems will not be adequately safeguarded to prevent unauthorized use, disclosure, and modification."

NIST has developed a guide on implementing an information security risk assessment process [NIST02]. The risk management methodology provided explains each step of the process and how each step fits into the system development life cycle (SDLC). The guide divides risk management into two main activities: risk assessment and risk mitigation. Through the risk management process defined in the guide, organizations will be able to better accomplish their missions by:

■ Securing the IT systems that store, process, or transmit organizational information

■ Enabling management to make well-informed risk management decisions to justify the expenditures that are part of an IT budget

■ Assisting management in authorizing (or accrediting) the IT systems on the basis of the supporting documentation resulting from the performance of risk management.

5.1.3 Evaluated Technology

Where appropriate, consideration should be given to using IT products that have undergone a formal security evaluation. Products that quarantine or block the behavior of active content are available on the market, and some have undergone formal evaluation. The focus of a formal security evaluation is primarily on the correctness and effectiveness of the design, under the well-founded principle that a sound design enables a secure implementation, while an unsound design is hopelessly doomed. Other, less formal forms of third-party testing and evaluation may rely on a set of functional and security tests. Many evaluations offer a range of assessment levels. For example, the NIST Cryptographic Module Validation Program (CMVP)[8] uses security evaluation levels defined in Federal Information Processing Standard (FIPS) 140-2 [NIST01]. Modules evaluated at Level 4 provide a higher level of assurance than those evaluated at Level 1. Nevertheless, an evaluated product without a needed security capability might be less desirable than a product having a lower level of assurance that offers the capability. A more detailed recommendation for Federal organizations on the acquisition and use of evaluated and tested products is available elsewhere [NIST00].

Note that using tested and evaluated software does not necessarily ensure a secure operational environment. The way in which a product is configured and composed with other system components affects security. Even when a product does successfully complete a formal security evaluation, it may contain vulnerabilities. For example, one of the most common attacks is through a buffer overflow, whereby the input to a defined programming interface is carefully crafted to overwrite memory beyond the input buffer limit with instructions designed to gain control of the process. Security evaluations might be expected to include a systematic search and elimination of buffer overflows; unfortunately, most do not. While evaluators test the implementation for known security vulnerabilities, and at more stringent levels even attempt penetrations, a systematic search of buffer overflow vulnerabilities is normally out of scope due mainly to cost. Automatic discovery of buffer overflow vulnerabilities within code is a research challenge.

5.1.4 Security Audit

A common approach for measuring the security posture of an organization is a formal security audit. Audits ensure that policies and controls already implemented are operating correctly and effectively. Audits can include static analysis of policies, procedures, safeguards, and configuration settings as well as active probing of the system's external and internal security mechanisms. The results of an audit identify the strengths and weaknesses of the security of the system and provide a list of noted deficits for resolution, typically ranked by degree of severity. Because the security posture of a system evolves over time, audits are most effective when done on a recurring basis.

While periodic formal audits are useful, they are not a replacement for day-to-day management of the security status of a system. Enabling system logs and reviewing their contents manually or through automated report summaries can sometimes be the best means of uncovering unauthorized behavior and detecting security problems. A well-known example of this is documented in Cliff Stoll's book, *The Cuckoo's Egg*, where a 75-cent accounting error appearing in a computer log eventually led to the discovery of an industrial espionage ring.

---

[8] More information about the NIST CMVP is available at http://csrc.nist.gov/groups/STM/index.html.

5.1.5 Application Settings

The desktop applications that handle active content documents typically have built-in controls that can be used to control or prevent access. For example, Apple's Safari, Mozilla's Firefox, and Microsoft's Internet Explorer Web browsers have options or preferences menus that can be used to select appropriate security settings regarding downloadable active content and mitigate risk [CERT06]. Most Web browsers provide pop-up blockers, which prevent Web sites from performing denial of service (DoS) attacks on a browser by overloading it with too many open windows. As of mid-2007, the major Web browsers incorporated phishing protection, which compares each Web site to a blacklist of known phishing Web sites before accessing it. Extensions are available to the Mozilla Firefox browser that strictly limit the use of JavaScript, Flash, and other active content technologies to trusted sites. Other browser-level security controls include providing safety ratings for all sites and links visited on the Web as well as supporting extended validation certificates that follow stricter issuing criteria.

The Security Configuration Checklists Program for IT Products hosted by NIST offers checklists that outline steps to lower the risks associated with Web browsers through tightly controlled configurations.[9] Email, spreadsheet, word processor, database, and presentation graphic desktop software applications have control settings similar to those of a browser and demand scrutiny in light of past exploits. For example, the ability of many email applications to render HTML-formatted content can be configured to disallow or disable any executable content, such as JavaScript. Tight functional binding among desktop applications is a concern, particularly where automatic rendering of multi-part or composite documents is enabled. Even today, products are often delivered with insecure default settings. Organizations deploying such applications must be familiar with the security options available to ensure they are used in accordance with organizational security policy.

5.1.6 Version Control and Patch Management

Administrators of systems can improve security by routinely applying security patches when they become available. Users and administrators can also take advantage of security enhancements to applications that they manage by upgrading to newer versions when appropriate. A comprehensive approach to patch management that addresses all applications involved with active content is essential, since unpatched flaws in ancillary products, including installed browser plug-ins, extensions, and helper applications, often leave systems open to attack.

Updating software products automatically over the Web is becoming increasingly popular, as the benefits are considerable. For example, users of recent versions of Windows can use built-in update features to find bug fixes and product updates and download them automatically. Using this feature requires the downloading of an ActiveX control that scans the computer for any needed updates particular to Microsoft software already installed. Other manufacturers have followed suit and provide update mechanisms for their own software. Many Web browsers, plug-ins, and extensions periodically check for new updates and notify the user. With the user's permission, updates can be installed automatically. As this practice becomes more commonplace, organizations should be aware of their implicit decision to allow a manufacturer to update software on their machines and act accordingly, following prescribed policy. NIST SP 800-40 Version 2.0, *Creating a Patch and Vulnerability Management Program* [NIST05] provides organizations with an overview of processes involved to efficiently patch systems across the enterprise.

---

[9] More information about the NIST checklist program is available at http://checklists.nist.gov/.

5.1.7 Isolation

Isolation can be applied at various levels. The simplest is complete isolation at the system level. A production computer system that is unable to receive active content documents cannot be affected by malicious hidden code. Although isolating a system physically is not always possible, logical isolation (e.g., via router settings or firewall controls) may be applied.

Virtualization takes logical isolation one step further, allowing multiple OSs to coexist on a computing platform. In virtualization, special purpose software successfully replicates the behavior of hardware. Through such methods, a single physical host computer can run multiple virtual machines, each with a distinct guest OS and associated applications. Various virtualization products exist that can be used to provide an isolated virtual machine environment for systems and applications to execute. Risky functions, such as Web browsing, may be confined to a virtual machine environment designated and configured exclusively for that purpose. This presumes that the virtualization software controlling the various virtual machine environments has adequate security [Gar07]. Should a virtual machine environment be compromised or become suspect, it can be replaced with the original version. Virtual machine technology is improving constantly. New versions of mainstream OSs are being designed with virtualization in mind and new x86 64-bit processors provide hardware-level support for virtualization.

Isolating tightly bounded, proprietary program components is another alternative. Seamless interoperation of products such as email, Web browsers, and office applications is a goal of product manufacturers. To provide better functionality or performance, manufacturers often allow products within their product line to take advantage of proprietary interfaces, which may not benefit from the widespread testing and scrutiny standard interfaces and protocols receive. By integrating products from different manufacturers, one can effectively induce those program components to use standard documented interfaces.

5.1.8 Minimal Functionality

Security is inversely related to complexity – the more complex a system, the more difficult it is to secure. Therefore, the functionality of a system should be reduced to the minimum needed to carry out its operation. Prudent users and administrators should remove unnecessary applications and program components to reduce complexity and shut off possible avenues of attack. Although a system configuration may have a function logically disabled, a clever attacker may be able to alter the settings to enable the functionality and then use it in an exploit.

On the browser side, unnecessary plug-ins or ActiveX controls should be removed. It is also recommended to substitute programs with lesser functionality in lieu of fully capable helper applications or plug-ins. Manufacturers of desktop applications often provide free software readers for electronic documents encoded in their proprietary file formats, for interpretation by recipients who do not own the application. Adobe Acrobat Reader, for example, allows users to view and print PDF files, but does not allow users to create or edit them. Since software readers are only intended to produce a viewable rendition of the document and have limited inherent capabilities, they eliminate many potentially harmful features and exploits based on implementation vulnerabilities contained in the full-fledged application. Besides manufacturer-provided readers, general-purpose software readers are commercially available that can render dozens of different file formats. A related measure is the selection of less capable types of active content documents, when multiple choices are available. Some Web sites offer an electronic document in a variety of formats such as proprietary word processor format, HTML markup, PostScript, or PDF. Users should take the opportunity to choose the most benign format for their operating environment.

On the server side, any unnecessary software not needed in providing Web services should be removed as well, particularly any development tools that could be used to further an attack if an intruder should gain an initial foothold. Ideally, server-side scripts should constrain users to a small set of well-defined functionality and validate the size and values of input parameters so that an attacker cannot overrun memory boundaries or piggy back arbitrary commands for execution. Scripts should be run only with minimal privileges (i.e., non-administrator) to avoid compromising the entire Web site in case the scripts have security flaws (see next subsection). Potential security holes can be exploited even when Web applications run with low privilege settings. For example, a subverted script could have enough privileges to mail out the system password file, examine the network information maps, or launch a login to an unknown service.

Whenever possible, content providers and site operators should provide material encoded in less harmful document formats. For example, if document distillers are not available to convert textual documents into PDF, an alternative is to make available a version in .rtf (rich text format), rather than a proprietary word processing format.

5.1.9   Least Privilege

The principle of least privilege states that programs should operate with only the privileges needed to perform authorized functions. During application development, it is easier to run code with all privileges, with the intention of paring back privileges in the production deployment. Unfortunately, privilege reduction is easy to overlook and often is. For example, Unix developers may enhance the server using Set-User-ID (SUID) programs, which refer to code that run with privileges of the owner (e.g., root) regardless of who is executing them. SUID programs, particularly those owned by root, can be dangerous because if subverted, they allow an intruder to gain control with the owner's privilege. Running the code instead with the minimum privileges needed restricts the range of access to the intruder, if an attack is successful. Similarly, on the browser side, any mobile code received should be constrained to the minimal privileges needed. For example, the Java security manager, part of the Java Runtime Environment of the browser, offers the user the ability to set fine-grained permission controls for incoming Java applets.

When applied to users, the principle implies that they should be assigned the minimum privileges necessary to perform their assigned tasks. For example, with Windows desktop systems, most users should be assigned to a rights-limited user group instead of one with full administrator rights. Such a constraint makes it more difficult for malware to install successfully and take effect, and also helps ensure only authorized applications are installed. To accommodate those users who at times require administrator rights, two separate accounts could be set up: an account with limited rights for performing daily tasks and an account with elevated rights for those exceptional times when administrator rights are needed to make configuration changes, install applications, and run applications that require higher privileges.

5.1.10 Layered and Diverse Defenses

Defending an information system requires safeguards to be applied throughout the system, as well as at points of entry. This principle is commonly called defense in depth. The selection and placement of security controls should be done in a way that progressively weakens or defeats all attacks. Having a series of similar controls in succession tends to only lengthen the duration of the attack. Applying different types of controls that complement each other and are mutually supportive is a much more effective approach. While the capabilities of available safeguards may overlap to some extent, the combined effect should exceed the effects of each control used individually. For instance, if control A misses 30% of attacks and control B also misses 30%, in combination they should only miss about 9% (.3

x .3) of attacks. A number of complementary technical safeguards, discussed in Section 5.2, are available, including classes of products that employ firewall, antivirus, intrusion detection, and behavior blocking technologies.

Manufacturers also provide a range of security controls that can be deployed on gateways and end-user systems, allowing organizations to more effectively layer defenses. For example, firewalls, intrusion detection and prevention systems (IDPS), and malware scanners are available at both the network perimeter and individual host levels.

5.1.11 Incident Response Handling

No matter how well an organization's security program is executed, inevitably a security breach will occur in a system. Besides adopting reasonable precautions for securing computer systems and networks, organizations must also establish the ability to respond quickly and efficiently when a security incident occurs. A security incident is a violation or imminent threat of violation of computer security policies, acceptable use policies or standard security practices that affects the confidentiality, integrity, or availability of a system or network. Examples of incidents include unauthorized use of an account, unauthorized elevation of system privileges, execution of malicious code that corrupts data or other code, DoS attacks, or a user providing illegal copies of software to others through file sharing services. Incidents may result in a partial or complete loss of security controls, an attempted or actual compromise of data, or the waste, fraud, abuse, loss, or damage of computational resources. Active content has played an increasingly significant role in security incidents, because of the additional attack surfaces exposed by each technology.

Responding to computer security incidents effectively necessitates a significant amount of preparation. Incident response activities require technical knowledge as well as effective communication and coordination among personnel who respond to the incident, to return the system as quickly as possible to normal operations. Proper periodic backup of critical files is a key ingredient in recovering from the adverse effects of an incident. NIST SP 800-61, *Computer Security Incident Handling Guide* [NIST04] provides an overview of the processes necessary for organizations to develop effective incident handling programs and policies.

5.2 Technical Safeguards

Appropriate technical controls need to be selected, deployed, and maintained as safeguards against malicious active content and mobile code. Four broad classes of technical controls have been identified, which can be summarized as follows [Rub98]:

■ **Filters** that examine code at points of entry and block or disable it if deemed harmful

■ **Cages** that constrain the code's behavior (e.g., privilege or function) during execution

■ **Signatures** that prevent code execution unless digitally signed by a trusted source

■ **Proofs** that define properties of code and are conveyed with it, which must be successfully verified before the code is executed.

Multiple instances of these controls can be combined to form hybrid safeguards. Further explanation is given in the following subsections.

5.2.1 Filters

Once forms of malicious content have been identified and understood, filtering can be used to detect and eliminate or completely block malicious content from entry. Many enterprise firewalls can filter email and Web pages for well-known file extensions and block them at the point of entry, following configured screening rules. More sophisticated ingress gateway filters can block or disable malicious code conveyed as active content. Desktop antivirus software has become increasingly capable of detecting active content having a malicious code signature. Client applications such as browsers, email, and word processors can also be configured to disable or ignore some forms of mobile code. Figure 5-1 gives a general overview of filtering performed on incoming active content, under the producer-consumer model presented earlier.

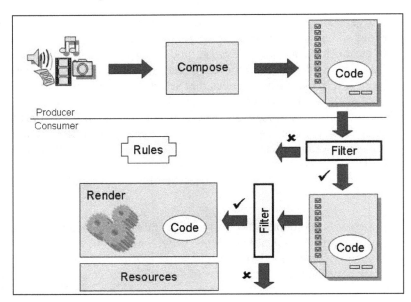

Figure 5-1. Filtering Incoming Active Content

Besides ingress filtering, egress filtering, which filters outgoing network traffic, is also useful in denying unacceptable actions originating from internal hosts. Strange or unexpected, but not necessarily unacceptable, transmissions from internal hosts may signal that they have been compromised in some way. Intrusion detection systems provide an additional safeguard for screening network and host behavior and provide notification when either inappropriate or unusual event sequences occur, or signatures of known exploits are matched.

While firewalls, antivirus software, and intrusion detection tools provide useful safeguards, they are not foolproof. Constructing a program to detect with certainty the presence or absence of harmful code within arbitrary programs or protocol is impossible. Moreover, a variety of techniques exists for deception such as mutation, segmentation, and disguise via extended character set encoding. Thus, filtering tools are faced with the prospect of diminishing returns – greater investments are needed for small increases in effectiveness. Despite services to refresh protection software with signatures of known exploits, and cascaded defense-in-depth measures, apart from total isolation there is no guarantee that something harmful cannot get through.

5.2.2 Cages

Nearly all interpretive execution environments, such as those supported by Web browsers and desktop applications, impose restrictions on the languages they process and execute. However, those restrictions may not be sufficient for all organizations. For such situations, imposing additional or redundant restraints on the code's behavior as it executes (e.g., privilege or function) might be appropriate. Conceptually, behavior controls can be viewed as a software cage or quarantine mechanism that dynamically intercepts and thwarts attempts by the subject code to take unacceptable actions that violate policy. Figure 5-2 illustrates the concept for the producer-consumer model.

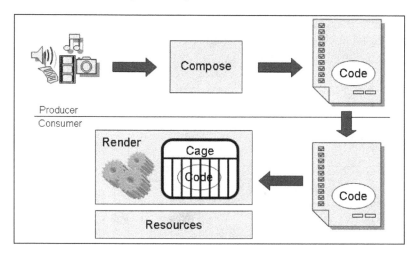

Figure 5-2. Constraining Active Content Behavior with a Software Cage

Many different approaches have been devised to thwart unwanted program behavior, including the following:

- Designing safe languages or eliminating unsafe commands from an existing language

- Running all code under policy enforced resource constraints

- Monitoring code activities and resource access

- Inspecting code and isolating the execution of harmful commands elsewhere

- Inspecting code and modifying or adding instructions to enforce policy.

These approaches manifest themselves in different ways in different products. Some language interpreters have a "safe" mode or limit functionality with a "padded cell" (e.g., Safe Tcl). Java confines code to a sandbox that prevents it from performing unauthorized operations. Finjan's behavior blocking products use a dynamic sandbox that subjects all active content to real-time monitoring and policy-based access control. Personal firewalls actively monitor and block network use.

As with firewall and antivirus products, technologies that dynamically restrain mobile code were born out of necessity to supplement existing mechanisms and represent an emerging class of security product. Such products are intended to complement firewall and antivirus products that block network transactions or mobile code based on predefined signatures (i.e., content inspection) respectively, and may refer to technologies such as dynamic sandbox, dynamic monitors, and behavior monitors used for controlling the behavior of mobile code [Vib01]. In addition to mobile code, this class of product may also be applicable to stationary code or downloaded code whose trustworthiness is in doubt.

5.2.3 Signatures

A digital signature is an unforgeable code computed over a document or other information that uniquely identifies the signer who computed it. When applied properly, a digital signature serves as a means of confirming the authenticity of an object, its origin, and its integrity. Because of these characteristics, digital signatures are involved in most authentication schemes. For example, the Secure Sockets Layer (SSL) protocol, built into most browsers and Web servers, relies on digital signatures for authenticating the parties involved in a transaction. When applied to mobile code, the code signer is typically the individual or organization that created the code. Figure 5-3 illustrates the general scheme.

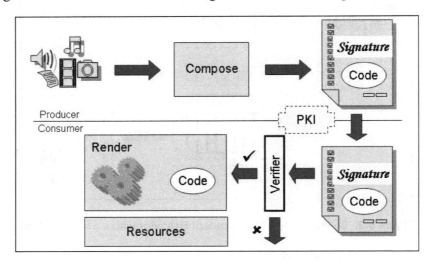

Figure 5-3. Verifying Active Content Digital Signatures

Digital signatures involve public key cryptography, which relies on a pair of keys associated with an entity. One key is kept private by the signing entity and the other is made publicly available. Passing mobile code through a non-reversible hash function provides a fingerprint or message digest of the code. Applying a digital signature function to the message digest using the private key of the signer forms a digital signature. A recipient uses the signer's public key to verify the signature conveyed with the code. The digital signature is in effect an integrity mechanism, since changes to the code would invalidate the signature and thus be detectable by the recipient. Digital signatures benefit greatly from the availability of a PKI, since certificates containing the identity of an entity and its public key (i.e., a public key certificate) can be readily located and verified. This allows the code, signature, and public key certificate to be forwarded to a recipient, who can easily verify the source and authenticity of the code.

When appropriate, digital signatures should be considered for use in applications involving active content, not only to verify the identities of the various parties involved, but also to confirm the integrity of any mobile code and the acceptability of the code's author. For example, Java can use digital signatures for determining the protection domain of downloaded code. Note that the meaning of a signature may be different depending on the policy associated with the signature scheme and the party who signs. For example, the author of some code, either an individual or organization, may use a digital signature to indicate who produced the code, but not to guarantee that the agent performs without fault or error.

Author-oriented signature schemes, such as Authenticode, were originally intended to serve as "digital shrink wrap", whereby the original product warranty limitations stated in the license remain in effect (e.g., the manufacturer makes no warranties as to the fitness of the product for any particular purpose). Many users misinterpret the significance of such a signature scheme beyond its original intent of establishing the authenticity of distributed software. Instead, it has become for the users a form of trust in the software's behavior, which could ultimately have disastrous consequences. The organization that issues trustworthy certificates can also be a potential source of problems. For example, an individual, posing as an employee of a well-known software manufacturer, was able to receive a class 3 software publisher certificate from a certification authority for Authenticode public key certificates [Ver01]. The successful deception demonstrated the possibility of malicious content being produced and distributed, which appears to come from a legitimate manufacturer.

5.2.4 Proofs

This technique obligates the code producer to provide formal evidence that the program possesses certain properties required by the consumer's policy (e.g., memory safety, access control, resource usage bounds). The best-known example of this technique is known as proof carrying code, in which the formal evidence is a proof of the safety properties of the code. The code and proof are sent together to the code consumer where the safety properties can be verified, as illustrated in Figure 5-4. The safety predicate must represent the semantics of the program to ensure that the companion proof does in fact correspond to the code. The proof should be structured in a way that makes it straightforward to verify without using cryptographic techniques or external assistance. Once verified, the code can run without further checking.

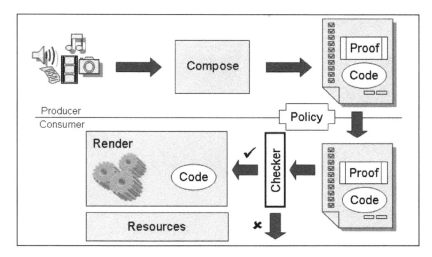

Figure 5-4. Verifying Proofs of Active Content Properties

Any attempts to tamper with the code or the safety proof result in either a verification error or, if the verification succeeds, a safe code transformation. The theoretical underpinnings of proof carrying code are based on well-established principles from logic, type theory, and formal verification. Nevertheless, some potentially difficult problems remain to solve before the approach is considered practical for widespread use.

5.2.5 Hybrids

It is also possible to combine more than one of the above classes of techniques to form a hybrid mechanism. For example, Java incorporates both cage and signature techniques in its security model. Model-carrying code is another example of a hybrid mechanism, which blends proof and cage techniques [Sek03]. It obligates the producer to generate a behavioral model of its program as formal evidence. Upon receipt, the consumer mechanically determines if the model conforms to security policies of interest. Rather than statically verifying the behavioral model, an enforcement model is generated from it for use by a runtime monitor (i.e., a behavioral sandbox). The runtime monitor is responsible for ensuring the execution of mobile code conforms to the enforcement model.

5.3 Safeguard Summary

This section presented the management, operational, and technical safeguards for mitigating risks associated with active content and mobile code described in Section 4. Safeguards are approved security measures taken to prevent or reduce the risk of system compromise. While a considerable number of safeguards exists, new techniques and refinements to existing ones can be expected as the use of active content technologies continues to increase and evolve.

6.   Summary

Active content offer benefits to both consumers and producers. The associated technologies are varied, yet sometimes similar and overlapping in function. Java applets, JavaScript, VBScript and ActiveX provide additional functionality to Web pages, while plug-ins, helper applications, and ActiveX controls enable browsers to support new types of content. PDF offloads the processing and interpretation of the presentation of documents to a display interpreter, and macros automate repetitive word processing and spreadsheet tasks. HTML, JavaScript, and Java are relatively platform independent and can run on many browsers. VBScript and JavaScript can also be used to pass information between HTML, Java, and ActiveX components. AJAX allows Web pages to be more responsive, akin to desktop applications.

The benefits of each of these active content technologies must be carefully weighed against the risks they pose. Security is not black or white, but shades of gray. When employing active content technology, security measures should be put in place to reduce risk to an acceptable level and to recover if an incident occurs.

Informed security officers, administrators, and other IT professionals are responsible for developing security policies based on their organization's specific security needs and level of acceptable risk. Unfortunately, rarely is there a "one size fits all" guideline that meets the unique needs of every organization. Thus, each organization must decide for itself what constitutes an acceptable level of risk and act accordingly. Establishing an organizational security policy is an important step in developing and applying appropriate security measures. The IT and security staff have a responsibility for keeping abreast of the risks associated with emerging technologies, by subscribing to security mailing lists and visiting manufacturer Web sites for information and updates to products used within their organization. As active content moves beyond desktop personal computers to mobile handheld devices, television sets, and other consumer electronic goods, users will be faced with competing and difficult tradeoffs of decreased privacy and security against increased functionality and ease-of-use.

Before handling active content documents, organizations should consider the following checklist, which summarizes some recommendations from the material presented in the previous sections:

- Develop the enterprise security policy regarding active content.

- Identify and assess the risk to critical information resources from active content.

- Audit systems on a regular basis to ensure the security policy is implemented correctly and remains effective.

- Identify critical information resources and maintain regular backups.

- Become knowledgeable of the security settings of desktop applications and turn off unneeded functionality.

- Keep systems current with the latest software upgrades and patches that address security vulnerabilities in desktop applications, such as Web browsers, readers, and email, and other critical software.

- Obtain all software through approved distribution channels, particularly through internal distribution channels set up by the organization for this purpose.

- Evaluate and install anti-malware software, firewalls, active content filters, and dynamic behavior monitors according to enterprise security requirements. Keep these products upgraded to the latest version.

- Read the fine print before agreeing to download application software and plug-ins.

- Institutionalize how needed plug-ins and other software code are obtained from software manufactures, evaluated, and distributed throughout the organization.

- Do not peruse active content or run downloaded software from untrusted sources. Enable ActiveX code only from trusted Web sites that require its use.

- Create and distribute active content documents only after carefully considering the risk and benefits.

- Consider using an isolated system and safe browser settings when visiting untrusted Web sites.

- Limit the applications installed on a system, deleting any that are not used or no longer needed.

- Disable JavaScript and any other active content processing capabilities within email desktop applications that are capable of handling HTML or other markup language encoded messages.

- Do not open active content documents or execute any email attachments without first verifying them with the sender. Be especially wary of attachments to electronic chain mails forwarded from or through friends.

- Keep informed of latest security advisories from the United States Computer Emergency Readiness Team (US-CERT) and the Computer Emergency Response Team (CERT) Coordination Center, and subscribe to security mailing lists.

- Periodically cross-check products against published lists of known vulnerabilities, such as the National Vulnerability Database (NVD),[10] that provide pointers to solution resources and patch information.

- Regularly audit systems and networks, quickly remedying any deficits noted.

- Know who to contact and what steps to take when discovering evidence of an intrusion.

One typical and common sense approach is to improve the security infrastructure incrementally over time. At each step, apply safeguards against the most critical risk items. For example, start with firewalls and gateway servers capable of screening active content and executable email attachments and successfully defending against a high percentage of Internet launched attacks. Later, for additional protection, complement antivirus software with behavioral controls, intrusion detection capabilities, or other technologies. Regular site security audits also help to identify vulnerabilities and appropriate safeguards, and to decide whether the remaining risks warrant further expenditures of time and money.

---

[10]   The NVD is hosted by NIST at http://nvd.nist.gov/.

7.   References

[Ado99]   *PostScript Language Reference*, third edition, Adobe Systems Incorporated, February 1999, http://www.adobe.com/products/postscript/pdfs/PLRM.pdf

[Ado07a]   Security Bulletin, Adobe Systems Incorporated, January 2007, http://www.adobe.com/support/security/bulletins/apsb07-01.html

[Ado07b]   *Adobe PDF Technology Center*, Adobe Systems Incorporated, January 2007, http://www.adobe.com/devnet/pdf/pdf_reference.html

[Anu98]   Anupam, V. and Mayer, A., *Secure Web Scripting*, IEEE Internet Computing, November/December 1998 (Vol. 2, No. 6), pp. 46-55

[Bec99]   Beck, K., *Embracing Change with Extreme Programming*, IEEE Computer, Oct. 1999 (Vol. 32, Issue 10), pp. 70 -77

[Bee07]   Beer, S., *Google manager: Google Apps replaced Microsoft Office at 100,000 businesses*, ITWire, February 23, 2007, http://www.itwire.com.au/content/view/9889/53/

[Bro04]   Brooks, R., *Mobile Code Paradigms and Security Issues*, IEEE Computer, May-June 2004 (Vol. 8, Issue 3), pp. 54-59, http://doi.ieeecomputersociety.org/10.1109/MIC.2004.1297274

[Car08]   Carr, Jim, *Attack Injects Malicious JavaScript into E-commerce Sites*, SC Magazine, January 15, 2008, http://www.scmagazineus.com/Attack-injects-malicious-JavaScript-into-hundreds-of-e-commerce-sites/article/104206/

[CERT06]   Dormann, Will and Rafail, Jason, Securing Your Web Browser, CERT Coordination Center, January 23, 2006, http://www.cert.org/tech_tips/securing_browser/

[CERT08]   Flash authoring tools create Flash files that contain cross-site scripting vulnerabilities, Vulnerability Note VU#249337, US-CERT, January 17, 2008, http://www.kb.cert.org/vuls/id/249337

[Cle90]   Van Cleef, Robert E., *New Roque Imperils Printers,* The Risks Digest, September 1990 (Volume 10, Issue 32), http://catless.ncl.ac.uk/Risks/10.32.html

[Clo01]   Clowes, Shaun, *A Study In Scarlet: Exploiting Common Vulnerabilities in PHP Applications*, SecureReality, 2001, http://www.securereality.com.au/studyinscarlet.txt

[CNET97]   *ActiveX Used as Hacking Tool*, CNET News.com, February 7, 1997, http://news.com.com/2100-1023-268947.html

[Coh95]   Cohen, Fred, *Internet Holes: 50 Ways to Attack Your Web Systems,* Management Analytics, 1995, http://all.net/journal/netsec/1995-12.html

[CSS1]   Cascading Style Sheets – level 1, W3C Recommendation, January 1999, http://www.w3.org/TR/1999/REC-CSS1-19990111

[CSS2]   Cascading Style Sheets – level 2, CSS2 Specification, W3C Recommendation, May 1998, http://www.w3.org/TR/1998/REC-CSS2-19980512/

[Cus99]   Cusumano, Michael A. and Yoffie, David B., *Software Development on Internet Time*, IEEE Computer, October 1999 (Vol. 32, Issue 10), pp. 60-69, http://csdl2.computer.org/persagen/DLAbsToc.jsp?resourcePath=/dl/mags/co/&toc=comp/mags/co/1999/10/rxtoc.xml&DOI=10.1109/2.796110

[Cza95]   Czajkowski, G. and von Eicken, T., *JRes: A Resource Accounting Interface for Java*, ACM Conference on Object Oriented Languages and Systems (OOPSLA), Vancouver, Canada, October 1998

[DoD06]   *Use of Mobile Code Technologies in Department of Defense (DoD) Information Systems*, DoD Instruction, October 23, 2006, http://www.dtic.mil/whs/directives/corres/html/855201.htm

[ECMA99]   *ECMAScript Language Specification*, 3rd edition, Standard ECMA-262, December 1999, http://www.ecma-international.org/publications/standards/Ecma-262.htm

[Fel97]   Felten, Edward W. et al, *Web Spoofing: An Internet Con Game*, National Information Systems Security Conference, October 1997, http://www.cs.princeton.edu/sip/pub/spoofing.html

[Fis01]   Fisher, Dennis, *'Peachy' Virus Targets PDF Files*, Interactive Week, August 8, 2001, http://www.verisign.com/support/advisories/authenticodefraud.html

[FTP]   Postel, J. and Reynolds, J., IETF Network Working Group RFC 959, *File Transfer Protocol (FTP)*, October 1985, http://www.ietf.org/rfc/rfc0959.txt

[Fug98]   Fuggetta, A., et al, *Understanding Code Mobility*, IEEE Transactions on Software Engineering, 24(5), May 1999, pp. 342-361, http://doi.ieeecomputersociety.org/10.1109/32.685258

[GAO07]   GAO-07-751T, *Information Security: Persistent Weaknesses Highlight Need for Further Improvement*, April 2007, http://www.gao.gov/new.items/d07751t.pdf

[GAO99]   GAO/AIMD-00-33, *Information Security Risk Assessment: Practices of Leading Organizations*, November 1999, http://www.gao.gov/special.pubs/ai00033.pdf

[Gar07]   *Rush to Virtualization Can Weaken Security*, Gartner Inc., Grid Today, April 3, 2007, http://www.gridtoday.com/grid/1349303.html

[Gil97]   Gilles, John, *Crackers Shuffle Cash with Quicken, ActiveX*, Wired News, February 7, 1997, http://www.wirednews.com/news/technology/0,1282,1943,00.html

[Gon98]   Gong, L., *Java Security Architecture (JDK 1.2)*, version 1.0, Sun Microsystems, October 1998, http://java.sun.com/j2se/1.4.2/docs/guide/security/spec/security-spec.doc.html

[Goo08a]   Goodin, Dan, *Google Researcher Calls for Flash Flush*, The Register, January 2, 2008, http://www.theregister.co.uk/2008/01/02/buggy_flash_fix/

[Goo08b]   Goodin, Dan, *Rogue ads infiltrate Expedia and Rhapsody*, The Register, January 30, 2008, http://www.theregister.co.uk/2008/01/30/excite_and_rhapsody_rogue_ads/

[Gos96]   Gosling, J. and McGilton, H., *The Java Language Environment: A White Paper,* Sun Microsystems, May 1996, http://java.sun.com/docs/white/langenv/

[Gro05]   Grosskurth, Allen and Godfrey, Michael, *A Reference Architecture of Web Browsers*, Proceedings of the 21st IEEE International Conference on Software Maintenance (ICSM'05), September 2005, pp. 661-664, http://grosskurth.ca/papers/browser-refarch.pdf

[Gro06]   Grosskurth, Allen and Godfrey, Michael, *Architecture and Evolution of the Modern Web Browser*, June 2006, http://grosskurth.ca/papers/browser-archevol-20060619.pdf

[Has00]   Hassan, Ahmed and Holt, Richard, *A Reference Architecture for Web Servers*, Proceedings of the Working Conference on Reverse Engineering (WCRE 2000), November 2000, http://www.bauhaus-stuttgart.de/dagstuhl/HassanHolt.pdf

[HTML4]   HTML 4.01 Specification, W3C Recommendation, December 1999, http://www.w3.org/TR/html4/

[HTTP]   Fielding, R., et al, IETF Network Working Group RFC 2616, *Hypertext Transfer Protocol – HTTP/1.1*, June 1999, http://www.ietf.org/rfc/rfc2616.txt

[Hug99]   Hughes, Paul, *Building a Web Browser*, THT Productions Inc., 1999

[IS15408]   ISO/IEC 15408:2005, Information technology -- Security techniques -- Evaluation criteria for IT security (Common Criteria), JTC 1/SC 27, 2005, http://www.iso.org/iso/en/CatalogueDetailPage.CatalogueDetail?CSNUMBER=40612

[Kei08]   Gregg Keizer, *Security pros: Kill ActiveX, Wave of IE plug-in bugs prompts US-CERT to recommend disabling ActiveX*, Computerworld, February 06, 2008, http://www.computerworld.com/action/article.do?command=viewArticleBasic&articleId=9061101

[Mar00]   Martin Jr., David et al, *The Privacy Practices of Web Browser Extensions*, Privacy Foundation, December 6, 2000, http://www.cs.uml.edu/~dm/pubs/bea.pdf

[McC03]   McCarty, Bill, *Botnets: Big and Bigger*, IEEE Security and Privacy, July-August 2003 (Vol. 1, No. 4), pp. 87-90, http://doi.ieeecomputersociety.org/10.1109/MSECP.2003.1219079

[MIME]   Borenstein, N. and Freed, N., IETF RFC 1521, *MIME (Multipurpose Internet Mail Extensions) Part One: Mechanisms for Specifying and Describing the Format of Internet Message Bodies*, September 1993, http://www.ietf.org/rfc/rfc1521.txt

[Mcl05]   McLellan, Drew, *Very Dynamic Web Interfaces*, O'Reilly Media Inc., February 9, 2005, http://www.xml.com/pub/a/2005/02/09/xml-http-request.html

[Mor98]   Morar, John F. and Chess, David M., *Web Browsers – Threat or Menace?,* Virus Bulletin Conference, October 1998, http://www.research.ibm.com/antivirus/SciPapers/Chess/Threat/Threat.html

[MS07]   Microsoft Security Bulletin Summary for June 2007, Microsoft TechNet Security Center, June 2007, http://www.microsoft.com/technet/security/bulletin/ms07-jun.mspx

[Nad07]   Nadir, Dan, *The Failure of URL Filtering in an Increasingly Dangerous Web World*, SC Magazine, September 19, 2007, http://www.scmagazineus.com/The-failure-of-URL-filtering-in-an-increasingly-dangerous-web-world/article/35696/

[NAM00]   NSTISSAM INFOSEC 3-00, *Advisory Memorandum on Web Browser Security Vulnerabilities*, August 2000, http://csrc.nist.gov/publications/secpubs/index.html#other

[Net06]   Netcraft, *PayPal Security Flaw Allows Identity Theft*, June 2006, http://news.netcraft.com/archives/2006/06/16/paypal_security_flaw_allows_identity_theft.html

[NIST00]   NIST SP 800-23, *Guidelines to Federal Organizations on Security Assurance and Acquisition/Use of Tested/Evaluated Products*, August 2000, http://csrc.nist.gov/publications/nistpubs/800-23/sp800-23.pdf

[NIST01]   Federal Information Processing Standard 140-2, *Security Requirements for Cryptographic Modules*, May 2001, http://csrc.nist.gov/publications/fips/fips140-2/fips1402.pdf

[NIST02]   NIST SP 800-30, *Risk Management Guide for Information Technology Systems*, July 2002, http://csrc.nist.gov/publications/nistpubs/800-30/sp800-30.pdf

[NIST04]   NIST SP 800-61, *Computer Security Incident Handling Guide,* January 2004, http://csrc.nist.gov/publications/nistpubs/800-61/sp800-61.pdf

[NIST05]   NIST SP 800-40 Version 2.0, *Creating a Patch and Vulnerability Management Program*, November 2005, http://csrc.nist.gov/publications/nistpubs/800-40-Ver2/SP800-40v2.pdf

[NIST07]   NIST SP 800-44 Version 2, *Guidelines on Securing Public Web Servers,* September 2007, http://csrc.nist.gov/publications/nistpubs/800-44-ver2/SP800-44v2.pdf

[OAA07]   *Ajax and Mashup Security*, An OpenAjax Alliance White Paper, September 13, 2007, http://www.openajax.org/whitepapers/Ajax%20and%20Mashup%20Security.html

[Pro07]   Niels Provos et al., *The Ghost In The Browser: Analysis of Web-based Malware*, Workshop on Hot Topics in Understanding Botnets (HotBots), April 10, 2007, http://www.usenix.org/events/hotbots07/tech/full_papers/provos/provos.pdf

[Pro08]   Niels Provos et al., *All Your iFRAMEs Point to Us*, Google Technical Report provos-2008a, Google Inc., February 4th, 2008, http://research.google.com/archive/provos-2008a.pdf

[Rub98]   Rubin, Aviel and Geer, Daniel, *Mobile Code Security*, IEEE Internet Computing, November-December 1998 (Vol. 2, No. 6), http://csdl2.computer.org/persagen/DLAbsToc.jsp?resourcePath=/dl/mags/ic/&toc=comp/mags/ic/1998/06/w6toc.xml&DOI=10.1109/4236.735984

[Sek03]   R. Sekar et al., *Model-Carrying Code: A Practical Approach for Safe Execution of Untrusted Applications*, ACM Symposium on Operating Systems Principles (SOSP), October 19–22, 2003, http://seclab.cs.sunysb.edu/seclab1/pubs/papers/sosp03.pdf

[Sha99]   Shankland, Stephen, *Melissa's Mischief Hits All Sides*, CNET News.com, March 31, 1999, http://news.com.com/2100-1023-223771.html

[SMTP]   Klensin, J. et al, IETF Network Working Group RFC 2821, *Simple Mail Transfer Protocol*, April 2001, http://www.ietf.org/rfc/rfc2821.txt

[Spe90]   Spencer, Henry, *Re: New Roque Imperils Printers*, The Risks Digest, September 1990 (Volume 10, Issue 35), http://catless.ncl.ac.uk/Risks/10.35.html

[SPI06]   SPI Dynamics, *AJAX Security Dangers*, 2006, http://www.sqlinjection.com/assets/documents/AJAXdangers.pdf

[Ste02]   Stein, Lincoln D., *The World Wide Web Security FAQ*, Version 3.1.2, February 4, 2002, http://www.w3.org/Security/Faq/www-security-faq.html

[Sun07]   Security Blog, Sun Microsystems, June 2007, http://blogs.sun.com/security/

[Ven99]   Venners, Bill, *A Walk through Cyberspace*, JavaWorld, December 1999, http://www.javaworld.com/javaworld/jw-12-1999/jw-12-jiniology.html

[Ver01]   *VeriSign Security Alert – Fraud Detected in Authenticode Code Signing Certificates*, March 22, 2001, http://www.verisign.com/support/advisories/page_030827.html

[Vib01]   Vibert, Robert, *AV Alternatives: Extending Scanner Range*, Information Security Magazine, February 2001, http://www.aladdin.com/about/press/esafe/InformationSecurity2-01.htm

[Wer99]   Werring, Laurentius, *The Hidden Threat Within*, 11th Annual Canadian Information Technology Security Symposium, May 1999, pp. 201-214

[XML1]   Extensible Markup Language (XML) 1.0, Second Edition, W3C Recommendation, October 2000, http://www.w3.org/TR/2000/REC-xml-20001006

[Zac03]   Zachary, John, *Protecting Mobile Code in the Wild*, IEEE Internet Computing, March-April 2003 (Vol. 7, No. 2), pp. 78-82, http://doi.ieeecomputersociety.org/10.1109/MIC.2003.1189192

Appendix A—HTTP Request Methods

Table A-1. Summary of Available Browser Request Methods

Method	Class	Meaning
OPTIONS	Probe	Get information about the communication options available
GET	Retrieval	Retrieve the resource identified by URL
HEAD	Probe	Retrieve meta-information (not content) about the identified resource
POST	Storage	Submit data to the identified resource
PUT	Create/Replacement	Upload a representation of the identified resource
DELETE	Removal	Delete the identified resource
TRACE	Diagnostic	Loop back this message
CONNECT	Server Error	Reserved for SSL tunneling via a proxy

Appendix B—HTTP Response Status

Table B-1. Categories of Server Response Code

Status Code	Class	Meaning
1xx	Informational	Request was received; continuing process
2xx	Success	The action was successfully received, understood, and accepted
3xx	Redirection	Further action must be taken to complete the request
4xx	Client Error	The request contains bad syntax or cannot be fulfilled
5xx	Server Error	The server failed to fulfill an apparently valid request

Appendix C—Glossary

Selected terms used in this publication are defined below.

Active Content: Electronic documents that can carry out or trigger actions automatically on a computer platform without the intervention of a user.

Attack: The realization of some specific threat that impacts the confidentiality, integrity, accountability, or availability of a computational resource.

Buffer Overflow: A condition at an interface under which more input can be placed into a buffer or data holding area than the capacity allocated, overwriting other information. Attackers exploit such a condition to crash a system or to insert specially crafted code that allows them to gain control of the system.

Cookie: A piece of state information supplied by a Web server to a browser, in a response for a requested resource, for the browser to store temporarily and return to the server on any subsequent visits or requests.

Interpreter: A program that processes a script or other program expression and carries out the requested action, in accordance with the language definition.

Macro Virus: A specific type of computer virus that is encoded as a macro embedded in some document and activated when the document is handled.

Malicious Code: A program that is written intentionally to carry out annoying or harmful actions, which includes Trojan horses, viruses, and worms.

Malware: A program that is inserted into a system, usually covertly, with the intent of compromising the confidentiality, integrity, or availability of the victim's data, applications, or operating system or of otherwise annoying or disrupting the victim.

Mobile Code: A program (e.g., script, macro, or other portable instruction) that can be shipped unchanged to a heterogeneous collection of platforms and executed with identical semantics.

Risk: A measure of the likelihood and the consequence of events or acts that could cause a system compromise, including the unauthorized disclosure, destruction, removal, modification, or interruption of system assets.

Safeguard: An approved security measure taken to protect computational resources by eliminating or reducing the risk to a system, which may include hardware and software mechanisms, policies, procedures, and physical controls.

Script: A sequence of instructions, ranging from a simple list of operating system commands to full-blown programming language statements, which can be executed automatically by an interpreter.

Scripting Language: A definition of the syntax and semantics for writing and interpreting scripts.

Spyware: A program embedded within an application that collects information and periodically communicates back to its home site, unbeknownst to the user.

Threat: A possible danger to a computer system, which may result in the interception, alteration, obstruction, or destruction of computational resources, or other disruption to the system.

Trojan Horse: A useful or seemingly useful program that contains hidden code of a malicious nature that executes when the program is invoked.

Virus: A program that replicates itself by attaching to other programs or files, where it hides until activated.

Vulnerability: A flaw or weakness in a computer system, its security procedures, internal controls, or design and implementation, which could be exploited to violate the system security policy.

Web Browser: Client software used to view Web content.

Web Bug: A tiny image, invisible to a user, placed on Web pages in such a way to enable third parties to track use of Web servers and collect information about the user, including IP address, host name, browser type and version, operating system name and version, and cookies.

Worm: A self-replicating program that propagates itself through a network onto other computer systems without requiring a host program or any user intervention to replicate.

Appendix D—Acronyms and Abbreviations

Selected acronyms and abbreviations used in this publication are defined below.

AJAX	Asynchronous JavaScript and XML
API	Application Programming Interface
ASCII	American Standard Code for Information Interchange
ASP	Active Server Pages
CERT	Computer Emergency Response Team
CGI	Common Gateway Interface
CLR	Common Language Runtime
CMVP	Cryptographic Module Validation Program
COM	Component Object Model
COTS	Commercial Off-the-Shelf
CSS	Cascaded Style Sheet
DNS	Domain Name System
DoD	Department of Defense
DoS	Denial of Service
ECMA	European Computer Manufacturers Association
FIPS	Federal Information Processing Standard
FISMA	Federal Information Security Management Act
FTP	File Transfer Protocol
GAO	Government Accounting Office
HTML	HyperText Markup Language
HTTP	HyperText Transfer Protocol
IDPS	Intrusion Detection and Prevention System
IEEE	Institute of Electrical and Electronics Engineers
IIS	Internet Information Services
IP	Internet Protocol
IPsec	Internet Protocol Security
ISAPI	Internet Server Application Programming Interface
IT	Information Technology
ITL	Information Technology Laboratory
Java EE	Java Enterprise Edition
JIT	Just-in-time
JSP	Java Server Pages
JVM	Java Virtual Machine
MIME	Multipurpose Internet Mail Extensions
MSIL	Microsoft Intermediate Language
NIST	National Institute of Standards and Technology
NSAPI	Netscape Server Application Programming Interface

NVD	National Vulnerability Database
OLE	Object Linking and Embedding
OMB	Office of Management and Budget
OS	Operating System
PDA	Personal Digital Assistant
PDF	Portable Document Format
PHP	PHP Hypertext Preprocessor
PKI	Public Key Infrastructure
PNG	Portable Network Graphics
SDLC	System Development Life Cycle
SMTP	Simple Mail Transfer Protocol
SP	Special Publication
SQL	Structured Query Language
SSI	Server Side Includes
SSL	Secure Sockets Layer
SUID	Set-User-ID
URI	Universal Resource Identifier
URL	Uniform Resource Locator
US-CERT	United States Computer Emergency Readiness Team
VB.NET	Visual Basic.NET
VBA	Visual Basic for Applications
VBScript	Visual Basic Script
WaSP	Web Standards Project
XML	eXtensible Markup Language
XSS	Cross-Site Scripting